Collins
revision guides

Total Revision

GCSE Business Studies

■ **Renée Huggett**

■ **Series editor: Jayne de Courcy**

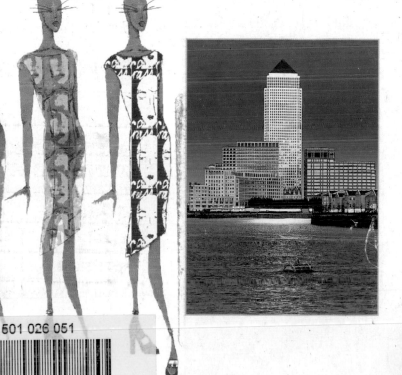

CONTENTS AND REVISION PLANNER

ABOUT THIS BOOK

Exams are about much more than just repeating memorized facts, so we have planned this book to make your revision as active and effective as possible.

How?

- by breaking down the content into manageable chunks (Revision Sessions)

- by testing your understanding at every step of the way (Check Yourself Questions)

- by providing extra information to help you aim for the very top grade (A* Extras)

- by listing the most likely exam questions for each topic (Question Spotters)

- by giving you invaluable examiner's guidance about exam technique (Exam Practice)

REVISION SESSION

Revision Sessions

- Each topic is divided into a number of **short revision sessions**. You should be able to read through each of these in no more than 30 minutes. That is the maximum amount of time that you should spend on revising without taking a short break.

- Ask your teacher for a copy of your own exam board's **GCSE Business Studies syllabus**. Tick off on the Contents list each of the revision sessions that you need to cover. It will probably be most of them.

? CHECK YOURSELF QUESTIONS

- At the end of each revision session there are some **Check Yourself Questions**. By trying these questions, you will immediately find out whether you have understood and remembered what you have read in the revision session. **Answers** are at the back of the book, along with **extra hints and guidance**.

- If you manage to answer all the Check Yourself Questions for a session correctly, then you can confidently tick off this topic in the box provided in the Contents list. If not, you will need to tick the 'Revise again' box to remind yourself to return to this topic later in your revision programme.

⚡ A* EXTRA

These boxes occur in each revision session. They contain some **extra information** which you need to learn of if you are aiming to achieve the very top grade. If you have the chance to use these additional facts in your exam, it could make the difference between a good answer and a very good answer.

QUESTION SPOTTER

It's obviously important to revise the facts, but it's also helpful to know how you might need to use this information in your exam.

The author, who has been involved with examining for many years, knows the sorts of questions that are most likely to be asked on each topic. She has put together these Question Spotter boxes so that they can help you to **focus your revision**.

Exam Practice

- This unit gives you **invaluable guidance on how to answer exam questions well**.

- It contains some sample students' answers to typical exam questions, followed by examiner's comments on them, showing where the students lost and gained marks. Reading through these will help you get a very clear idea of what you need to do in order to score full marks when answering questions in your exam.

- There are also some **typical exam questions** for you to try answering. Model answers are given at the back of the book for you to check your own answers against. There are also examiner's hints, highlighting **how to achieve full marks**.

- Working through this unit will give you an excellent grounding in exam technique. If you feel you want further exam practice, look at *Do Brilliantly GCSE Business Studies*, also published by Collins Educational.

About your Business Studies course

All GCSE Business Studies syllabuses and examinations:

- test your knowledge;

- test your ability to apply knowledge;

- test your skill in selecting information and drawing conclusions from it.

Knowledge

This book provides a simple and clear summary of the essential knowledge for success in Business Studies, with detailed explanations of more complicated topics where necessary. It is also extremely useful for students taking Applied Business examinations, as it provides practically all the background material they need.

Topics covered

This book covers all the main topics in the syllabuses of the GCSE Examination Boards. However, some boards have optional subjects in the examination or in the coursework element. Check with your teacher which topics you need to study and revise for your exam.

Foundation and Higher tier

There are two levels, or tiers, in the examination: the Higher tier for Grades A* to D, and the Foundation tier for Grades C to G. The same topics are covered in both levels of the examination, and the same case studies are sometimes used for both. The main difference is that there are more short, point-marked questions in Foundation-tier papers, and more open-ended questions, with level-of-response marking, in the Higher-tier papers.

Grading

This book will help you to improve your grade by:

- giving plenty of practice in dealing with case-study material;

- showing the difference between point marking and level-of-response marking;

- describing what examiners want when they use key command words such as 'explain' or 'describe';

- warning you about some of the most common errors that candidates make in their answers.

UNIT 1: BUSINESS FUNDAMENTALS

Production

⊞ Needs and wants

- All businesses exist to satisfy **needs** and **wants**. There are five basic needs that are essential for our existence: water, food, shelter, clothes and warmth.

- However, in addition to these five basic needs, we have dozens of different wants, which are increasing all the time. People want to travel to foreign countries, to have well-equipped sports centres, to have instant treatment for any illness, to name just a few.

- Our idea of needs and wants is always changing. For example, we could live without a television, a video recorder, a telephone or a washing machine, but practically all homes have them now. As a result, they have become an essential part of modern life, a modern need and no longer a want.

⊞ Goods and services

- Modern business has responded to our increased wants by providing literally thousands of different kinds of **products** for us to buy. There are two main types of product: **goods** and **services**. Goods are physical objects that we can see and touch, such as a football. Services are non-physical products, such as education or gardening. There are three main kinds of goods:

  1 **Non-durable goods** are goods, provided mainly for **consumers**, which do not last very long, as they are used almost as soon as they are bought, for example food.

  2 **Durable goods** are those which last much longer and will be kept until they break, wear out or are replaced, such as cars and furniture.

  3 **Organizational, or industrial, goods** are goods which are supplied to other firms or organizations to help them to make the goods they produce.

⊞ Factors of production

- Four factors of production are involved in making every product. They are:

  1 land (including the sea)

  2 labour (the physical and mental efforts of workers)

  3 capital (the plant and machinery which allows workers to do their jobs)

  4 enterprise (the skills of **entrepreneurs** who can see business opportunities and take the risk of exploiting or using them)

- All of these factors are in short supply, either because there is a natural shortage or because the resources are in the wrong place or of the wrong kind.

⚡ A* EXTRA

The terrorist attacks on New York and Washington on 11th September 2001 and the subsequent military action in Afghanistan provide examples of how consumer needs and wants can be altered by outside events. Many businesses were affected by these events, from airlines, as more people avoided flying, to financial institutions, as people sold shares, fearing they would lose their money.

1.1 *Durable and non-durable goods and services*

Non-durable goods   *Durable goods*

Organizational goods   *Services*

THE MANY USES OF LAND

- Land is used to grow food, graze animals and grow trees. The land also contains a variety of natural substances, such as oil, gold, iron ore, sand and clay, which are used to manufacture goods.

- Although it might appear that there is a surplus of land, much of it cannot be used because it is uncultivated rainforest, desert or permanently covered by ice. There may be a great surplus of land which no one particularly wants in some parts of the country, such as the Scottish islands, but a great scarcity of land in other places, such as the centre of Birmingham or London.

SCARCITY OF LABOUR

- Labour, however, is mobile, as people can go and work in different parts of Britain or in foreign countries where workers are wanted. However, there is still a shortage of labour, which is increasing all the time.

SHORTAGES OF CAPITAL AND ENTREPRENEURS

- Capital or capital goods, such as factories, machinery and vehicles, are also in short supply. Many factories and machines are old fashioned and inefficient.

- Entrepreneurs who can pick the most profitable opportunities and raise the money to exploit them are always scarce.

1.2 *Four factors of production*

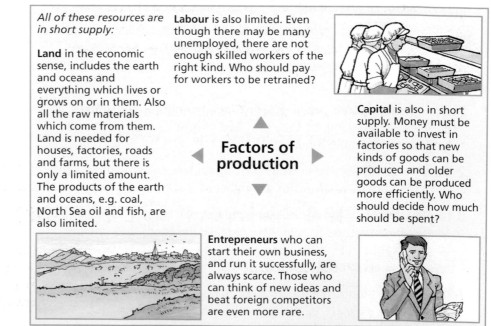

All of these resources are in short supply:

Land in the economic sense, includes the earth and oceans and everything which lives or grows on or in them. Also all the raw materials which come from them. Land is needed for houses, factories, roads and farms, but there is only a limited amount. The products of the earth and oceans, e.g. coal, North Sea oil and fish, are also limited.

Labour is also limited. Even though there may be many unemployed, there are not enough skilled workers of the right kind. Who should pay for workers to be retrained?

Factors of production

Capital is also in short supply. Money must be available to invest in factories so that new kinds of goods can be produced and older goods can be produced more efficiently. Who should decide how much should be spent?

Entrepreneurs who can start their own business, and run it successfully, are always scarce. Those who can think of new ideas and beat foreign competitors are even more rare.

⊞ Changing proportions of four factors

- The relative importance of each factor of production is changing all the time. Currently there is a change from a **labour-intensive industry** to a **capital-intensive industry**, which will eventually become even more marked as computer-controlled robots are used to do more and more of the physical work. In a similar way, the amount of land needed by farmers falls as they become more efficient at growing food.

⊞ Kinds of production

- To make the best use of these limited resources, businesses specialize in the kind of work they can do best. There are three main kinds of **production**:

  1 primary (meaning first)

  2 secondary (meaning second)

  3 tertiary (meaning third)

PRIMARY PRODUCTION

- Primary production supplies the raw material from which other goods are made. Mining, quarrying and extractive industries provide metals, precious stones, fuels and building materials; the farming and fishing industries provide raw materials for food and drink; and forestry provides timber.

SECONDARY PRODUCTION

- Secondary production uses these raw materials to make finished goods. (Note that the building and construction industry and the **utilities**, which supply water, gas and electricity, are included in this category.)

TERTIARY PRODUCTION

- Tertiary production supplies services of all kinds for all the other businesses, the government and consumers. The tertiary sector is the biggest sector of production and it is still increasing in size. There are three main kinds of services:

  1 **personal services**, such as the professional services of teachers, doctors, dentists and lawyers, and **transport services** by road, rail and air

  2 **commercial services**, such as retailing, distribution and advertising

  3 **financial services**, both for consumers and for the other two sectors

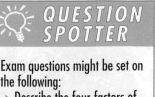

QUESTION SPOTTER

Exam questions might be set on the following:
▶ Describe the four factors of production.
▶ What is an entrepreneur? Explain how entrepreneurs contribute to the success of a business.
▶ State the three types of production and give an example of each.

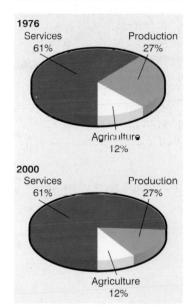

1.3 *Percentages employed in different sectors in 1976 and 2000*

? CHECK YOURSELF QUESTIONS

Q1 What is the difference between non-durable and durable goods? Give one example of each.

Q2 Give the meanings of the following terms and one example of each:

  a capital

  b primary production

Q3 Look at Figure 1.3. By what percentage (to the nearest whole number) did the number of people working in the services sector increase between 1976 and 2000?

Answers are on page 151

Production chains and markets

⊞ What is a chain of production?

- All three sectors of production – primary, secondary and tertiary – are linked together in a **chain of production**. All businesses are interdependent. The furniture maker would have no raw materials without the forester. The forester would have a much smaller market without the furniture maker. The retailer is dependent on the furniture maker for his or her supplies. Without retailers, furniture makers would have a much smaller market, as they could sell their products only locally. Each of them adds value to the product as it passes through their hands, i.e. their work makes it more valuable than it was before.

⊞ Increasing specialization

- In all sectors of production, there is an increasing amount of specialization. For example, many firms no longer distribute their own goods. It is cheaper and more efficient to hand the job over to a specialist firm of distributors.

- In a similar way, car manufacturers no longer make the whole car themselves. They buy in different parts from various suppliers and then assemble them to make the finished product. In some cases, engines are made in one country, the body in a second country and the car is assembled in a third country.

⊞ Involvement of other sectors

- Other sectors are involved in this process. All of these firms rely on banks to provide them with capital to finance their business. The customers who buy the finished products may have taken out a bank loan to buy their car, or bought it on hire purchase through another kind of firm. The government raises money through taxes to finance the building of the roads on which the cars will travel. The firm that builds the roads will need to buy cars and other vehicles of its own to carry out its work.

⊞ The purpose of markets

- A **market** is a means of putting buyers and sellers in touch with one another so that goods or services may be bought and sold.

TRADITIONAL MARKETS

- Originally, markets were physical places, such as fairs or crossroads in the countryside. This kind of general market selling a great variety of goods still exists in weekend street markets, collectors' fairs and car-boot sales.

MODERN MARKETS

- Most modern markets are highly specialized, and the buyers and sellers do not have to meet.

- The range of goods and services is now so great that there are literally thousands of markets of different kinds. A brief glance through the Yellow Pages will give some indication of the variety.

1.4 *An extract from the Yellow Pages*

⊞ Private and public sectors

- The great majority of businesses in the Yellow Pages are in the **private sector**. These businesses range in size from small firms with just one owner to huge companies, such as Marks & Spencer, which is owned by thousands of **shareholders**.

- Some other goods and services, however, are provided by the **public sector** – the government and local councils. For example, the government provides the National Health Service, while councils provide a wide range of services, such as home helps and libraries.

- In addition, there is a **voluntary sector**, composed of charities that provide a targeted service for specific sections of the community in need of help. For example, Shelter helps the homeless and other people with housing problems.

MIXED ECONOMY

- Like most developed countries, Britain has a **mixed economy**, which is composed of these three separate sectors – private, public and voluntary. Until fairly recently, the public sector was very much bigger than it is today. But, from 1979 onward, many of the firms that were once owned by the government were transformed into private companies owned by their shareholders.

- Examples of **privatization** are BT, British Airways and the electricity, gas and water companies. In addition, the private sector is now increasingly encouraged by the government to provide some public services, such as health care and prisons.

? CHECK YOURSELF QUESTIONS

Q1 a What is a mixed economy?

b In which part of a mixed economy might the following be employed?
  i) car factory worker
  ii) nurse
  iii) Oxfam manager
  iv) hairdresser
  v) statistician

Q2 What is the meaning of 'market'?

Answers are on page 151.

UNIT 2: KINDS OF BUSINESS

Sole proprietors

⊞ Advantages of being a sole proprietor

■ The majority of businesses in Britain are owned by **sole proprietors**. Sole proprietors are found in all three sectors of production, but over 60 per cent are in the tertiary sector.

■ The main advantage of being a sole proprietor is that you are in complete control of the business and can run it just the way you like. It is also very easy to set up the business. There are no complicated legal procedures. Your only obligation is to keep proper business accounts for the Inland Revenue and to keep VAT (value added tax) accounts when your annual sales exceed a certain limit.

■ Another big advantage is that with many kinds of self-employment, you need only a small amount of capital to start.

■ Sole proprietors keep all the **profit** of the business (the difference between the amount of money a business receives and all the costs of running it). The business is also very flexible. If one product is not working well, it is much easier to switch to another product than it would be in a big firm.

■ Most sole proprietors also obtain great **job satisfaction**. They really like what they are doing and gain pleasure when they succeed.

⊞ Disadvantages of being a sole proprietor

■ There are also disadvantages. The main one is **unlimited liability**. This means that sole proprietors are personally responsible for all the debts and losses of the business. If they cannot pay their way, they may have to sell their home and all their possessions to pay their bills.

■ Other disadvantages are:

• It is often difficult to raise money to expand a sole proprietor's business.

• The business may collapse if the owner is ill or dies, and it cannot be passed on to another person.

• There is often no one to help if things go wrong.

• There is usually great competition, so the risks of failure are high.

PROFIT
Owner retains

RISK
High

CONTROL
Total

2.1 *A sole proprietor*

⚡ A* EXTRA

Sole proprietors can reduce risks by obtaining relevant experience and knowledge of the business first and by seeking advice from high-street banks, trade associations and Business Links.

▦ Personal qualities needed

- You need certain qualities to succeed as a sole proprietor. Some of the most important are:

  - persistence

  - enthusiasm

  - ability to work hard

  - willingness to take risks

  - organizational skills

  - tolerance and patience

- Even if you have all of these qualities, it is still no guarantee of success. The greatest failure rate is among people who have very little experience of the job – or even none at all – and hope to pick up knowledge as they go along.

QUESTION SPOTTER

Exam questions might be set on the following:
- State two advantages and two disadvantages of being a sole proprietor.
- Explain the legal requirements of a solo proprietor.

? CHECK YOURSELF QUESTIONS

Q1 State two personal qualities that a sole proprietor should have.

Q2 Why would a cheese shop be an appropriate kind of business for a sole proprietor?

Answers are on page 152.

Partnerships

PROFIT
Shared

RISK
Medium

CONTROL
Shared

2.2 *A partnership*

▦ What is a partnership?

■ A **partnership** is a form of business which is owned and controlled by the partners. Legally, a partnership can have up to 20 partners, though some professionals, such as solicitors, are allowed to have more. Professional persons, such as solicitors, accountants, doctors and architects, are most likely to form partnerships.

■ Legally, any two or more persons carrying on a business for profit together are partners, even if no documents have been signed. Their partnership is then governed by the Partnership Act of 1890.

■ **Sleeping partners** take no active part in the business, but invest money or lend their name to the partnership. They share in the profits and are also responsible for any debts.

▦ Advantages of partnerships

■ The main advantage of a partnership is that each partner can specialize in a particular area so that the firm provides a better service. In a firm of solicitors, for example, one partner might specialize in criminal law and another in property. Partners are able to do their own work without having total responsibility for running the whole business.

■ As more people are involved in a partnership, it should produce more profitable ideas than a single individual. It should also be easier to raise capital, as there are more people to contribute to the initial outlay.

▦ Disadvantages of partnerships

■ Like the sole proprietor, partners have unlimited liability. The main drawback is the greater risk of conflicts between the partners. Some of the most common disputes are caused by:
  • the sharing of profits
  • the control of the business
  • the responsibilities of the various partners
  • perceptions that one partner may not be pulling his or her weight

▦ Deed of partnership

■ The Partnership Act of 1890, which governs partnerships unless there is a separate written agreement, does not provide solutions to the numerous disputes and problems that can arise. Therefore it is essential to have a solicitor draw up a legal **deed of partnership**. The most important matters it should cover are:
  • the amount of capital each partner should provide
  • how profits (and losses) should be divided between partners
  • whether all partners have only one vote
  • the rules for taking on new partners
  • how the partnership could be dissolved, or one partner could withdraw.

QUESTION SPOTTER

Exam questions might be set on the following:
▸ What kind of businesses might be suitable for a partnership?
▸ Explain some of the main disadvantages of a partnership.
▸ Describe the relative advantages of sole ownership of a business compared with a partnership.

⊞ Worker co-operatives

- A **worker co-operative** is a firm which is owned and controlled by the whole **workforce** (all the people who work there). There are around 1,500 worker co-operatives in the UK. They are most common in catering, engineering, farming, printing and dressmaking. Most of them are small, with only a dozen or so members.

MANAGEMENT AND FINANCE

- Co-operatives are all run in a democratic way, with each member, regardless of their job, having one vote. However, in some cases, the members make only the policy decisions and a paid manager runs the company on a day-to-day basis.

- The co-operative is financed by the members' own money or by grants. Profits are distributed to members in a 'fair' way, not necessarily in proportion to the amount of money invested.

BENEFITS AND DRAWBACKS OF WORKER CO-OPERATIVES

- The main advantages of worker co-operatives for their members are:
  - a great sense of involvement, as the business belongs to the workforce
  - a feeling of equality, as each member has one vote
  - greater job satisfaction, as people feel they are working for themselves

- The main disadvantages are:
  - difficulty in reaching decisions, as everyone has a vote regardless of whether they have any knowledge or experience of the matter involved
  - failure to be competitive
  - profit may be sacrificed to ideas
  - financial control is often weak unless a manager or accountant is employed
  - difficulty in raising finance

- Worker co-operatives are a very small part of the wider co-operative movement, with its Co-op and Leo convenience stores and supermarkets. Co-operative Retail Societies, which have over eight million members, are run on the same principles of co-operative sharing rather than private profit. There is also a Co-operative Bank, a Co-operative Insurance Society, Co-operative Travel and other businesses.

❓ CHECK YOURSELF QUESTIONS

Q1 What is a sleeping partner?

Q2 State two items that might be found in a deed of partnership and explain why they are included.

Answers are on page 152.

Franchising

⊞ What is franchising?

A* EXTRA

Franchisers usually run a pilot scheme first to see if the idea would be practical and profitable. They set up a training programme and advertise for franchisees. If the franchiser decides to go ahead with the scheme, it is then advertised nationally.

- **Franchising** is another form of co-operation between the **franchiser** (a firm which allows a person to trade under its name and to sell its product for a fee) and the **franchisee** (someone who pays the firm for the privilege of being allowed to sell its tried-and-tested product).

- Franchising appeals to people who want to run their own business without facing all the risks and problems of the sole proprietor. There are nearly 600 franchises, with a **turnover** (or total sales) of £7.4 billion a year.

- Many of the best-known high-street names, such as McDonald's, Wimpy, Body Shop and Prontaprint, are franchise operations.

⊞ Setting up a franchise system

A* EXTRA

In addition to full business-format franchises, there are also many exclusive dealerships in which manufacturers give another business the exclusive right to sell their products in a particular area. These dealerships are common with cars, computers, beer, etc. The total value of this market is about eight times bigger than that of franchising.

- A legal contract will be drawn up between the franchiser and the franchisee covering all aspects of the business relationship, including:

  - the total capital that the franchisee must invest

  - the amount of **royalty** payments – the percentage payment which the franchisee has to pay the franchiser on every sale, which is usually around ten per cent

  - the length of time the franchise will last

  - the method of withdrawing from the franchise or disposing of it to another person

  - the initial and ongoing support that the franchiser will provide

  - where the franchisee should buy supplies for the business

⊞ Advantages and disadvantages

FOR FRANCHISERS

- The main advantages for franchisers are:

  - they can expand their business without investing large amounts of money

  - risks are reduced because they are shared with the franchisee

  - regular royalty payments are received from franchisees

  - franchisees are usually more ambitious and hard-working than some employees

  - most franchised businesses are profitable

- The main disadvantages for franchisers are:
  - the company's trade name – and reputation – can be ruined if franchisees do not maintain standards

  - the initial costs of the trial operation

  - ongoing costs of national advertising and support of franchisees

FOR FRANCHISEES
- The main advantages for franchisees are:

  - they have a much bigger chance of succeeding than a sole proprietor, as their product is already successful and has a secure place in the market

  - banks are usually more willing to lend money to a franchisee

  - the franchisee benefits from continuous support from the franchiser. If there are any problems, the franchiser may often know the answer straight away, as similar problems may have occurred with other franchisees

- The main disadvantages for franchisees are:

  - less independence than a sole proprietor

  - continuing royalty payments

  - may not be able to sell the business without the franchiser's approval

  - sometimes tied into buying all supplies, at higher prices, from the franchiser

CHECK YOURSELF QUESTIONS

Q1 What is a franchiser?

Q2 Describe the term 'royalty payment'.

Q3 What are the main differences between a sole proprietor and a franchisee?

Answers are on page 153.

Limited companies

QUESTION SPOTTER

Exam questions might be set on the following:
▸ What is the meaning of:
a) dividend; b) shareholder;
c) liquidation?
▸ Explain the term 'limited liability'.
▸ Why has limited liability made it possible for modern businesses to develop and expand?

⊞ What is a limited company?

■ A **limited company** has a totally different structure from any other kind of business. In all the businesses described so far, the owners are all actively involved in running the business whether they are a sole proprietor, a partner, a member of a worker co-operative or a franchisee. (Sleeping partners are the only exception.)

■ In a limited company, however, ownership and work are separated. The business is owned by **shareholders**, who have bought a number of ordinary shares in the company and receive a share of its profits. The business is run by the **directors** of the company and paid employees. The directors are often, although not always, shareholders.

⊞ Limited liability

■ Companies are called 'limited' because the shareholders, or owners, have **limited liability**. Their financial liability is limited to the amount of money they have invested.

■ A company might be making so little profit that it could not pay its way and is forced to stop trading by going into **liquidation**. The company might be millions of pounds in debt, but the shareholders would not be responsible. They might lose the money they have invested in shares, but not a penny more.

■ Limited liability is the foundation of modern business. It encourages people to invest their money in businesses, in return for which they hope to receive high **dividends** (a share of the profits which are paid out to shareholders every six months or once a year).

■ Limited companies pay a different kind of tax from people – **corporation tax** instead of income tax – and **business rates** instead of domestic rates.

■ Because a company has a separate legal identity, it does not end with the death of shareholders. Even if all of them died, their shares could be sold to other people and the company would survive.

⚡ A* EXTRA

Before a company can be set up, it has to provide the Companies Registration Office with a memorandum of association stating the nature of the business and its share capital, and articles of association saying how often shareholders' meetings will be held and how the company will be organized.

⊞ Disadvantages of limited companies

■ There are some disadvantages of being a limited company:
  ● It is more complicated to set up a limited company than it is to start a business as a sole trader. A company has to be registered with the Companies Registration Office.
  ● It is also more expensive, as it is usually necessary to employ a solicitor to register the company.
  ● The company's accounts have to be sent to the Companies Registration Office every year, where the public may inspect them.

- With big companies, the accounts also have to be approved by an **auditor**, trained in checking accounts, which makes it even more expensive.

Private and public limited companies

- There are two kinds of companies: **private limited companies** and **public limited companies**. A private limited company has the abbreviation 'Ltd' (standing for 'limited company') after its name; a public limited company has 'plc' (standing for 'public limited company').

- Shares in a private company cannot be advertised for sale to members of the general public. They can only be sold privately. All the shareholders have to agree to the sale.

PUBLIC LIMITED COMPANIES

- A plc is usually bigger than a private limited company. It must have a minimum of £50,000 share capital.

- Shares are sold to members of the public through banks, stockbrokers or firms that deal in shares.

- The **nominal value** of each share when first issued may be only 25p or £1, but the shares are traded on the Stock Exchange, where their price can rise or fall dramatically in accordance with the company's current fortunes.

- Privatizations and the conversion of building societies into plcs have increased the number of private shareholders.

- Most shares are owned by **institutional investors**, such as insurance companies, pension funds and banks with many millions of pounds to invest.

QUESTION SPOTTER

Exam questions might be set on the following:

▸ State two differences between an independent company and a franchise.
▸ Describe the different kinds of shareholders.
▸ Explain the main differences the directors of a private company would find if the company became a plc.
▸ State some of the major factors which might cause a private company to become a plc.

A* EXTRA

The number of private investors has also increased because of the development of the Internet. This provides individual investors with authoritative data and company information. Many of these private investors are speculative day traders who buy and sell shares in a single session in the hope of making an instant profit.

? CHECK YOURSELF QUESTIONS

Q1 What is the nominal value of a share?

Q2 State *two* differences between a public limited company and a private limited company.

Answers are on page 154.

UNIT 3: OBJECTIVES AND ORGANIZATION

REVISION SESSION 1

The need for profit

What is profit?

■ In the private sector, the main objective of all businesses is to make a **profit**. Profit is the difference between the **turnover** of a business (the money it receives from the goods or services that it sells) and its **operating costs** (all the money that it spends on running the business).

3.1 *Turnover, profit and costs*

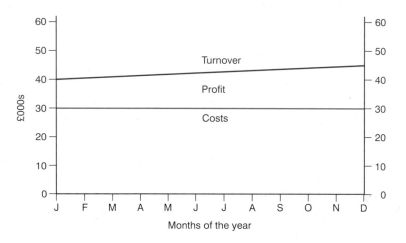

A* EXTRA

The term 'turnover' is used in three different ways. Here, it is used to indicate the value of sales over a period of time. It is also used to measure the number of times a business replaces its stock in a year (stock turnover), and the rate at which employees leave a business each year (labour turnover). The latter is expressed as a percentage.

■ If a business did not make a profit, it could not survive for long, as it would be spending more money than it received. A business needs to make a profit to pay:
  • suppliers
  • interest charges on money it has borrowed
  • its employees
  • its taxes
  • a dividend to shareholders (if it is a company)

Other benefits of profit

■ Profits also provide many other benefits for business and for the economy as a whole:
  • Profits encourage businesses to become more efficient by cutting costs.
  • Increased profit helps to finance the expansion of a business.
  • The hope of profits encourages people to invest in existing businesses and to start new ones.
  • Profit also stimulates businesses to take risks. For example, pharmaceutical companies spend millions of pounds every year developing new drugs in the hope of finding one wonder drug that will sell all over the world.
  • In a wider sense, profit helps to make business responsive to consumer demand.

A* EXTRA

Profit is the main driving force of modern economies. If consumers do not buy a product in sufficient quantities, the business will stop producing it and replace it with something else. In Britain, consumer spending accounts for about two-thirds of total expenditure.

Profit and the public sector

- Up until the end of the 1970s, the public sector was not expected to make a profit. At best, it was expected to cover all its costs (break even). If it did not do so, the government would usually give it a **subsidy** – a grant from public funds – to keep it going.

- Most government subsidies have now been abolished, except for some essential services such as suburban commuter rail services, inner-city development and job creation.

GOVERNMENT-SET FINANCIAL TARGETS

- Organizations that remain in the public sector are expected to meet strict financial targets, to break even and to pay for any necessary new investment or persuade the private sector to help pay for it.

Profit maximization

- Although all private-sector businesses have to make a profit to survive, they can also have other **objectives** – particular aims that a business is trying to achieve. Some businesses may want to make the highest possible profit – **profit maximization**.

- For example, sole proprietors may want to make as much profit as possible so that they can obtain the status symbols of success. On the other hand, some highly skilled sole proprietors, such as stained-glass makers or wrought-iron workers, gain so much satisfaction and pleasure from their work that they are content to make just enough profit to live on.

- A larger company may want to make the highest possible profit so that people will want to buy the new shares it is going to issue. However, these companies do not always make profit maximization their main objective. They may need to keep their prices low – and therefore reduce their profits – so that they can enter a new market or compete more fiercely with their rivals.

QUESTION SPOTTER

Exam questions might be set on the following:
- Give two motives for profit maximization.
- Describe the objectives of the public sector.
- Explain how the objectives of one plc has changed over time.

CHECK YOURSELF QUESTIONS

Q1 What is turnover?

Q2 Explain the term 'profit'.

Q3 Look at Figure 3.1 on page 14, which shows the turnover and costs of a business. By what percentage did the profits increase during the year?

Answers are on page 154.

Other business objectives

QUESTION SPOTTER

Exam questions might be set on the following:
▸ State two business objectives apart from profit.
▸ Give two examples of work which might be outsourced by a big corporation.
▸ Explain why businesses are constantly updating their products.

⊞ Cutting costs

■ Competition between firms is now so fierce that all businesses have to keep costs low so that they can match or beat their rivals' prices. One of the main ways of doing this is by reducing the number of employees.

One way of reducing labour is by **outsourcing** some of the work or paying a specialized firm to do it.

3.2 Turnover and costs This graph shows how profit increases as costs are cut.

⊞ Introducing new products

■ One of the main strengths of a business is its products. If a business is to succeed in an increasingly competitive world, it must constantly update its products and develop new ones.

⊞ Satisfying customers

■ At one time, most businesses were **product oriented**. A manufacturer's main concern was to make a high-quality product which was better than its rivals' and which would last a lifetime.

■ Practically all modern businesses are **market oriented**. Their main concern is to make products that customers want.

■ Manufacturers still want to make high-quality products which are better than their rivals', but they are more concerned with satisfying their customers' changing wants than permanent needs.

■ Many businesses now put customer satisfaction at the top of their 'other objectives' list. They really try to find out what customers want and satisfy their wants so that they become regular, loyal customers.

⊞ Increased market share

■ **Market share** is the percentage of a total market that a product, or a company, holds. It is sometimes measured by volume, so that a cider manufacturer, for example, could calculate his or her share of the total British market by the number of units, or bottles, sold. However, it is usually measured in value of sales in pounds. The company with the greatest market share is the **market leader**.

⚡ A* EXTRA

Satisfying customers is now such a vital aspects of all businesses that manufacturers in the industrial goods sectors involve major customers in the research, design and production of new equipment from the start to ensure that their requirements are taken into account. If the main clients contribute to the development of new products, they are far more likely to buy the finished product, as it will have been 'tailor made' for them.

- Market share is one of the best measures of success as a high market share shows that a business is performing more effectively and efficiently than its competitors. The firm benefits because it will be able to borrow money more easily from banks and raise more money from investors.

🏢 Expanding the business

- Another major objective might be to increase the size of a business. The size of a company can be measured by:

  - turnover, or total sales

  - the number of employees

  - the amount of capital (the amount of money invested in the business)

  - the stock market value, which is calculated by multiplying the current share price by the number of shares issued

- These criteria measure only size, not efficiency. A company could increase its turnover, but its costs might rise so that its profit falls.

🏢 Opportunity cost

- If a business wants to expand or develop new products, it will often have to sacrifice part of its profit to do so. For every choice that a business makes, there is always an **opportunity cost** – some other alternative that must be sacrificed or given up.

- Opportunity cost is one of the basic principles underlying all business decisions. For example, if a shopkeeper decides to have his or her shop repainted, he or she may not be able to afford new carpets for the shop.

SACRIFICE OF ALTERNATIVES

- Opportunity cost is not expressed in money terms, but in the sacrifice of the next best alternative. In the shopkeeper's case, the opportunity cost of repainting the shop was the sacrifice of the next best alternative – buying carpets.

- The same principle applies to the government, which spends about 40 per cent of the wealth that is produced in Britain every year. Should it build new roads or hospitals? Should it spend more on retraining and education or more on inner cities?

? CHECK YOURSELF QUESTIONS

Q1 Describe the main differences between a product-oriented firm and a market-oriented firm.

Q2 How does a firm benefit by increasing its market share?

Answers are on page 155.

Scale and mergers

⊞ Economies of scale

■ Bigger businesses gain some enormous advantages over smaller businesses through economies of scale. As a firm grows in size, its costs will fall owing to internal **economies of scale**. The main economies are:

1 **Technical economies:** Big manufacturers that make goods in huge quantities can use mass-production methods. These break the production process into a large number of small tasks that can be carried out by separate groups of specialized workers.

2 **Buying economies:** Big firms can buy raw materials, components and other goods in bulk, and can therefore get a discount, or a lower price, from the supplier.

3 **Marketing economies:** The cost of advertising products is spread over a larger number of units. Advertising is, therefore, relatively cheaper than in smaller firms.

4 **Financial economies:** It is easier for big firms to borrow money because of their greater financial security. They can also borrow money more cheaply, as their size gives them the power to bargain with lenders. The sources of finance are wider, too, as plcs can raise money by issuing shares.

5 **Administrative economies:** The costs of management in big firms are also proportionately lower, as they are spread over a larger volume of production.

6 **Distribution economies:** Big firms can use their transport more efficiently by carrying larger loads, or they can outsource this operation to a specialist distribution firm.

7 **Risk-bearing economies:** Big companies usually operate in several markets and often in different countries. This **diversification** reduces their risks as they are less likely to be affected by a slump or fall in demand in one market or one country.

(For external economies of scale, see page 138.)

⊞ Mergers and takeovers

■ One of the main ways in which a business can expand is through a **merger** with another company, when they become one firm. Sometimes, one firm – Company A – will **take over** another firm – Company B – by buying a majority of the shares from the present shareholders.

FRIENDLY AND HOSTILE TAKEOVERS

■ Most takeovers are friendly, with the directors of Company B supporting the takeover and advising shareholders to sell. Occasionally, however, the takeover bid is hostile and is resisted by the directors of Company B.

⚡ A* EXTRA

About half of all mergers of big corporations ultimately fail. Some of the main reasons are executive rivalries, clash of corporate cultures, and divided aims and loyalties. Some spectacular failures have occurred in the telecommunications industry.

MAKING EMPLOYEES REDUNDANT

- Mergers and takeovers produce economies of scale, as there is usually some duplication of work in the two firms. Costs can be reduced by closing down sections, or even whole departments, and making employees **redundant**.

ASSET-STRIPPING

- With very big companies that own several different kinds of business, any unwanted businesses can be sold off. Some of the company's assets – the things that it owns, such as property – may also be sold off quickly to raise more money. This is known as **asset-stripping**.

⊞ Kinds of mergers

- There are five main kinds of merger:

  1 horizontal

  2 lateral

  3 vertical backwards

  4 vertical forwards

  5 conglomerate

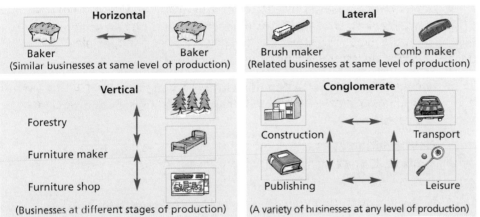

3.3 *Mergers and takeovers*

HORIZONTAL MERGERS

- A horizontal merger is when a firm merges with another firm that makes the same product, e.g. two small bakers or two large aircraft manufacturers.

- The main advantages are:

  - economies of scale

  - greater market share

  - opportunities for more specialization

  - reduction in competition

  - obtaining skills and knowledge of specialist staff

  - gaining goodwill of other business

  - easier to raise money

QUESTION SPOTTER

Exam questions might be set on the following:
- What is a conglomerate?
- Explain the difference between a horizontal and a lateral merger.
- How would a brewer benefit by taking over a chain of public houses?

LATERAL MERGERS

- A lateral merger is the joining together of two firms with similar products that do not compete directly with each other, e.g. a bank and a building society.

- The main advantages are:
  - economies of scale
  - diversification, or spreading risks over different kinds of business
  - easy entry into new market
  - obtaining use of specialist staff or skills and knowledge

VERTICAL BACKWARDS MERGERS

- A vertical backwards merger occurs when a firm joins with another firm in the same industry which is further back in the chain of production. For example, a furniture manufacturer (secondary sector of production) might buy a forester's business (primary sector of production), or a chain of shoe shops (tertiary sector) might buy a shoe manufacturer (secondary sector).

VERTICAL FORWARDS MERGERS

- This occurs when a firm merges with another firm at a later stage in the chain of production. For example, a brewer (secondary sector of production) might take over a chain of pubs (tertiary sector).

- Sometimes, a business integrates all three sectors. For instance, oil companies often do their own production, refining and selling.

CONGLOMERATE MERGERS

- When firms with completely different products merge, it is called a conglomerate merger. A **conglomerate** is a large company with a variety of businesses producing many different kinds of goods and services.

? CHECK YOURSELF QUESTIONS

Q1 Give an example of a vertical backwards merger.

Q2 Describe how big firms benefit from two economies of scale.

Q3 Don Bartlett is a baker with his own small shop. He has just taken over a nearby sandwich shop, which sells mainly to local office workers and college students.

  a What kind of takeover was it?

  b What is the main benefit for Don Bartlett?

Answers are on page 155.

Organizational structures

田 Organization charts

- Sole proprietors have to do all the work of organizing their business themselves. It is much more difficult to organize a big company, with thousands of employees on many different sites.

- **Organization charts** like Figure 3.4 (sometimes called 'organigrams') show the usual way in which a big manufacturing company might be organized.

3.4 *An organization chart*

Chairperson

Managing Director

Production Manager | Marketing Director | Sales Manager | Personnel Manager | Financial Director

Purchasing Manager | Technical Manager | Quality Control Manager

Levels of authority

CHAIRPERSON

- The firm shown in Figure 3.4 is organized as a **hierarchy**, with the most important and powerful person, the **Chairperson** of the board of directors, at the top. The chairperson helps to decide the policy of the firm with his or her fellow directors, who are elected by the shareholders to help run the company.

MANAGING DIRECTOR

- The **Managing Director** is in charge of the day-to-day running of the business. (Note: in many non-manufacturing firms, the managing director is now called the **chief executive**.)

EQUAL AUTHORITY

- The next most powerful people in the firm are the five departmental managers. (Note: because their work is so important to the organization, the Marketing Director and the Financial Director are also members of the board of directors, as their titles show.) The five departmental heads have an equal amount of authority, so they are on the same level of the hierarchy.

> ⚡ **A* EXTRA**
>
> A manager who has authority over a group of managers is known as their 'line manager' because she or he is immediately above them in the chain, or line, of command.

CHAIN OF COMMAND

■ The Managing Director has authority over the five departmental managers. This creates a clear **chain of command**, showing the line along which orders and decisions are passed down to people who are lower in the hierarchy.

■ The Production Manager has authority over the three **senior managers** in his department – the Purchasing Manager, the Technical Manager and the Quality Control Manager. There would be other **middle managers** in the production department below them. (The other departments would also have their own senior and middle managers.)

■ If there are only a few levels in the hierarchy, there will be a short chain of command. The more levels there are, the longer the chain of command.

SPAN OF CONTROL

■ Each person in a hierarchy has a certain number of people to whom he or she can give orders and who report directly to him or her. For example, the Managing Director has five people, or **subordinates**, immediately below him in the hierarchy, therefore his **span of control** is five. The Production Manager's span of control is three.

■ The width of the span of control depends on the following factors:

- Kind of work: Simple work needs less supervision, so the span of control can be wide.

- Communications: Subordinates who are a long way from their superiors – on a different site or even in a foreign country – may be more difficult to control.

- Level of skills: If both the manager and the subordinates are good at their jobs, because they have great skills and experience, there can be a wide span of control.

- Delegation: Some managers are more willing to delegate some of their powers to subordinates by letting them do some of the manager's jobs, enabling the manager to have a wider span of control.

⊞ Advantages and disadvantages of delegation

■ **Delegation** is when a superior gives a subordinate, or an employee of lower rank, the authority to carry out a specific duty or duties.

■ The main advantages are that it:

- saves the manager's time

- makes subordinates' work more interesting

- gives subordinates valuable experience

- speeds up decision-making

■ The possible disadvantages are that it:

- takes up more of the manager's time initially

- increases the chance of mistakes

- needs some way of checking that tasks have been done

⊞ Division of labour

■ One of the main advantages of the hierarchical system is that the organization's structure is firmly based on a **division of labour**, with each department performing one main task. Within each department, individual employees also specialize in one particular task or tasks.

⊞ Functions of departments

■ The main function, or work, of each **department** in an organization is:

- **Production department:** controls production process and purchasing of parts; maintains quality of goods; keeps costs low; maintains production schedule.

- **Marketing department:** identifies the needs and wants of customers and provides goods or services to satisfy them; finds suitable markets; helps to promote and advertise products.

- **Sales department:** sells products to customers; deals with any complaints; sometimes organizes distribution of goods.

- **Personnel department** (sometimes called the Human Resources department): is in charge of everything to do with employees, including recruitment, training, wages, salaries; plays a big part in industrial relations.

- **Finance department:** obtains, analyses and records organization's finance; makes sure that money is used to the best advantage.

⊞ Advantages of hierarchies

■ Organizations with a hierarchical structure based on function have advantages for both employers and employees.

■ The main advantages for employers are:

- Specialized staff work more efficiently.

- The clear chain of command improves communications.

- Each employee has only one immediate superior, which produces **unity of command**.

- It is easy to check that work has been done properly as there are managers or supervisors at all levels of the hierarchy.

- Co-operation is easier, as managers can speak for all the employees they control.

■ The main advantages for employees are:

- They know who their boss, or line manager, or supervisor, is.

- They receive orders only from their own manager or supervisor

- It is easy to get help from experienced colleagues in their own section or department.

- Being in a section or a department gives them a greater sense of unity and purpose.

QUESTION SPOTTER

Exam questions might be set on the following:
▸ What are the chief functions of the main departments in a manufacturing firm?
▸ Why are most organizational structures based on function?
▸ Where would you expect to find a narrow span of control?

⊞ Disadvantages of hierarchies

■ Some of the main disadvantages of the hierarchical system of management are:

- There may be great rivalry between departments.

- People may become too specialized and do not see the whole picture.

- Senior managers may put the interests of their departments before those of the firm.

- Incompetent or bullying heads of department can cause havoc in their department.

- The hierarchical system is often rigid and inflexible.

- The long chain of command makes communications more difficult.

- Power comes from a person's standing, or level, in the hierarchy, not necessarily from their competence.

⊞ Other organizational structures

■ The structure of most organizations is based on function because the advantages are bigger than the drawbacks. But some organizations also include other elements in their structure:

1 geographical

2 market

3 product

GEOGRAPHICAL

■ A firm making farm machinery and equipment might include a geographical element in its structure, because the needs of arable farmers in East Anglia differ from those of sheep farmers in Devon.

MARKET

■ An insurance company might include a market element in its organization to cater for the separate markets for its products – domestic insurance, business insurance, car insurance, life assurance.

PRODUCT

■ A vehicle manufacturer might include a product element in its structure to cater for cars, vans and lorries.

? CHECK YOURSELF QUESTIONS

Q1 What is the main advantage of having separate departments in a large firm?

Q2 What are the disadvantages of a long chain of command?

Q3 When would you expect to find a wide span of control?

Answers are on page 156.

REVISION SESSION 5 — Problems of multinationals ◼ UNIT 3

⊞ Organizational Problems

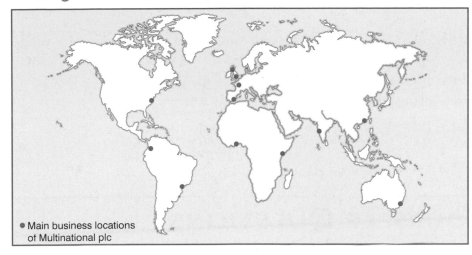

- Main business locations of Multinational plc

3.5 *A multinational's global operations*

- **Multinationals** – large companies which operate in a number of countries – have special organizational problems because they often produce a large number of products. Should their organization be based on function, geography, market or product?

- They also have another organizational problem. Should there be a large amount of **centralization**, where the parent company retains most power, or **decentralization**, where a large amount of authority is delegated to subsidiary companies?

  - Centralization gives great buying, technical and financial economies of scale, and decisions are more likely to be based on the interests of the whole business.

  - Decentralization speeds decision-making and responses to changes in local conditions.

- In practice, the parent company usually retains control of general policy, the appointment of top managers and finance. Some big groups expand overseas by franchising.

⊞ Diseconomies of scale

- Managing really big companies is so difficult that it may produce **diseconomies of scale**, which cause inefficiency and a rise in costs.

- Some of the main reasons are:

  - The parent company may not keep in touch with all its markets.

  - There may be disputes and rivalries between the parent and subsidiary companies.

  - There may be too many managers, which increases costs and makes it more difficult to make decisions.

  - The managers become too inflexible, or fixed, in their attitudes.

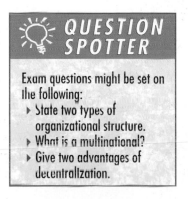

⚡ A* EXTRA

The disadvantages of centralization are the long chain of communication, remoteness of central authority, slow feedback and lack of authority in branches. The disadvantages of decentralization are lack of a general strategy, conflicts between the central and subsidiary authority, fewer economies of scale.

💡 QUESTION SPOTTER

Exam questions might be set on the following:
- ▸ State two types of organizational structure.
- ▸ What is a multinational?
- ▸ Give two advantages of decentralization.

- Employees lose motivation to work hard because they may feel they are just a company number, not an individual.

■ Although big companies have much more money, power and authority, small businesses are still able to compete because they have some natural advantages:

- They are far more flexible and can respond to their customers' wants and needs more quickly.

- They are more willing to experiment because they often retain an entrepreneurial spirit.

- They can provide a more personal service than a large company.

- They are able to gain a firm hold of niche markets.

? CHECK YOURSELF QUESTIONS

Q1 Name two diseconomies of scale and their effects.

Q2 Why do some multinational retailers use franchises in their overseas markets?

Answers are on page 157.

UNIT 4: FINANCE

Costs and budgets

⊞ Capital and revenue expenditure

■ It is essential for all businesses to control their costs.

■ Costs can be divided into two main categories, **capital expenditure** and **revenue expenditure**:

• Capital expenditure is the money that is spent in setting up a business or in buying long-term assets.

• Revenue expenditure is what is spent on running the business from day to day.

⊞ Fixed and variable costs

■ Revenue expenditure can also be divided into two main kinds:

• fixed costs

• variable costs

■ Questions about these two terms often come up in exams, so it is essential that you understand the differences between them.

■ **Fixed costs** (or **overheads**) are those costs which do not change in the short term and have to be met whether the business is profitable or not. They include such items as rent, rates, interest charges, repayments of loans, insurance and salaries.

■ **Variable costs** are costs which vary according to the amount of work being done or goods being produced or sold. They include such items as raw materials, fuel and power, and wages.

■ When these costs are shown on a graph, the fixed costs are shown as a straight line, as in Figure 4.1. The variable costs are shown as a sloping line above the fixed costs and therefore shows the total costs, as it includes both the fixed costs and the variable costs (see Figure 4.2).

⊞ Semi-variable costs

■ Not all costs fit neatly into these two categories of fixed and variable. There are also **semi-variable costs**, which means that they are fixed up to a certain level of production, but variable after that point is reached.

MANAGEMENT COSTS

■ Management costs are one example. The office staff in a factory might be able to cope with the increased paperwork if output rose by ten per cent. But if it increased by 50 per cent, more office staff would have to be employed.

> ⚡ **A* EXTRA**
>
> Costs can also be classified as direct costs, such as wages, salaries, raw materials and components, and indirect costs, such as overheads.

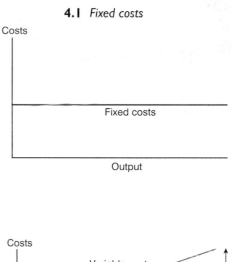

4.1 *Fixed costs*

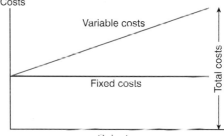

4.2 *Variable and fixed costs*

Exam questions might be set on the following:
▶ What are a) fixed costs; b) variable costs; c) semi-variable costs?
▶ If a manufacturer's output increased by five per cent, how might the fixed and variable costs be affected?

A* EXTRA

The term 'budget' is also used for the annual government statement in which the Chancellor of the Exchequer describes in detail how much money the government expects to raise in the coming financial year from taxes and other receipts and how much money it expects to spend.

REPAIR COSTS

■ Repairs are another example. A machine might keep going for a few more months without being repaired, but if production suddenly increased it would probably break down unless it was repaired.

COSTS OF ELECTRICITY

■ Electricity costs are particularly complicated, as they can be both a fixed cost and a variable cost.

■ When electricity is used to heat the offices in a factory, it is a fixed cost, because this has to be done whether the factory is making any goods or not. But when it is used to power the machines in the factory, it is a variable cost, because the amount used will vary in accordance with the amount of goods produced.

■ In addition, electricity is also a semi-variable cost, as there is a fixed standing charge that must be paid whether any power is used or not, and a variable charge that increases with the number of units used.

⊞ Budgets

■ To ensure that their costs are kept firmly under control, businesses make out a budget for the year ahead.

■ Each department makes out its own budget showing what it hopes to achieve in the next year and its forecast costs. These are not just guesses but detailed factual and financial statements of what is going to be spent and what is going to be achieved month by month, or quarter by quarter, during the following year.

■ When they have been agreed, all the budgets are put together to make a master budget for the whole firm.

BUDGETARY CONTROL

■ Budgets have three main purposes:

1 They set definite, short-term objectives for each department and the whole firm.

2 They provide financial targets, such as a reduction in costs of two per cent.

3 They provide a means of assessing performance, as monthly or quarterly targets can be checked against actual results.

■ If there is a large difference between the forecast target and the actual result, the causes can be investigated and appropriate action can be taken. This is known as **budgetary control**.

⊞ Cutting costs

■ Businesses can cut their costs in various ways. Some of the main ways are:

- move to cheaper premises

- stop non-vital insurance

- carry out only essential repairs and maintenance

- reduce training programmes

- find new suppliers with lower prices

- cut advertising expenditure

- stop employing new staff

- reduce part-time employees' hours of work

- cut managers' expense accounts

■ It is necessary to make sure that these cuts do not reduce the efficiency of a business, as this could produce even greater problems.

? CHECK YOURSELF QUESTIONS

Q1 Give one example of a variable cost and one example of a fixed cost.

Q2 A self-employed artist/designer with a rented studio had the following costs for one month: rent £80; paint, paper, canvas, etc. £70; business rates £50; models' fees £85; interest on bank loan £25; travel £35; post and packing £30; heat, light and power £40.

a What were the total costs?

b How much were the fixed costs and the variable costs?

c What percentage were the fixed costs and the variable costs of the total costs?

Q3 Why is it important for a business to have a budget?

Answers are on page 157.

Cash and cash flow

⚡ **A* EXTRA**

You need to distinguish between debit cards, where money is withdrawn immediately from the account to which the card relates, and credit cards, where payment does not have to be made until some weeks after the transaction.

💡 *QUESTION SPOTTER*

Exam questions might be set on the following:
▸ State one advantage for a business of using cash to pay bills.
▸ A large company has accumulated large reserves of cash. What effects might this have on the performance of the company?

▦ What is cash?

■ **Cash** is an asset, or something that a business owns, which is liquid, or immediately available for paying bills. There are two kinds of cash.

1 **Cash in hand** consists of money in the till or cashier's office and petty cash, which is kept in the office to pay for immediate expenses, such as taxi fares.

2 **Cash at bank** is the money in a current account in a bank or building society which allows customers to withdraw money immediately or pay by cheque or a debit card, such as Switch.

■ There are also other funds that are just as liquid as cash, such as instant-access **deposit accounts** in banks or building societies from which money can be withdrawn immediately.

▦ Non-liquid assets

■ **Non-liquid assets** cannot be used immediately to pay bills. However, some are more liquid than others.

■ Assets that are nearly liquid include:

• investments in other firms which can usually be sold immediately, though payment will not be received for some days

• funds in term deposit accounts, where notice of a certain number of days has to be given before the money can be withdrawn

■ Some other assets are less liquid.

• Debtors are other businesses or individuals who owe money to the firm, but they do not always pay their debts on time.

• Stock is finished goods that are waiting to be sold. Profit would be sacrificed if they were sold off cheaply to pay the business's debts.

• Fixed assets, such as land, buildings, machinery or vehicles, would usually have to be sold at a loss if they were disposed of quickly to raise cash.

▦ Cash-flow forecasts

■ To guard against the problems caused by a shortage of cash, businesses make out a **cash-flow forecast** for the year ahead. This forecasts the amount of money that will flow into the business (the receipts) and the amount that will flow out (the payments) for each month of the year. It covers all kinds of **cash inflow**, including sales, loans, grants and new money invested in the business, and all kinds of **cash outflow**, including both revenue and capital expenditure.

- Figure 4.3 shows a simplified cash-flow forecast for three months.

- In March, the business had £5,000 in the bank. Its cash outflow exceeded the inflow by £1,000, which reduced the bank balance to £4,000.

£s	March	April	May
Cash inflow	97,000	74,000	79,000
Cash outflow	98,000	73,000	87,000
Opening bank balance	5,000	4,000	5,000
Closing bank balance	4,000	5,000	(3,000)

4.3 *A simplified cash-flow forecast*

- The following month, the position was reversed, with cash inflow being £1,000 more than cash outflow. This restored the bank balance to £5,000.

- In May, the outflow exceeded the inflow by £8,000 (£87,000 – £79,000 = £8,000), which used up all the money in the bank and left a deficit of £3,000 (shown in brackets).

- The business in Figure 4.3 above is tottering on the brink of disaster all the time. It would need to examine in great detail all the individual items in its budget and actual amounts of payments and receipts to see what was going wrong.

Managing cash flow

- A big multinational, such as BP, uses colour-coded charts to show its cash inflow from its normal business and the fluctuations caused by exceptional events, such as the payment of a tax bill in Alaska.

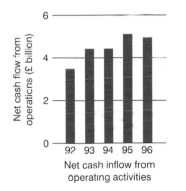

Net cash inflow from operating activities

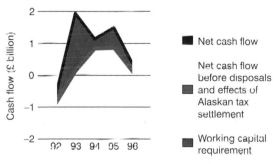

■ Net cash flow

Net cash flow before disposals
■ and effects of Alaskan tax settlement

■ Working capital requirement

4.4 *BP's cash-flow charts*

- How can a business deal with a cash-flow crisis? Some solutions are:

  - ask for an increased overdraft from the bank

  - try to reschedule debts by asking the bank manager to allow a longer time for repayment of a loan

  - reduce cash spending by buying more on hire purchase or on credit

  - limit payment time for debtors

  - allow credit only over a specific amount

  - try to increase sales. If prices are reduced, the loss of revenue might be compensated for by much higher turnover

  - reduce costs by buying cheaper materials, delaying repairs, etc.

  - reduce staff where no redundancy payments would be involved

CHECK YOURSELF QUESTIONS

Q1 What is the difference between liquid and non-liquid assets?

Q2 John works from home as a self-employed gardener. His main work is cutting lawns and hedges. His only assets are his lawnmower, a hedge-cutter and a ten-year-old van. He advertises in several local shops from time to time and has an advertisement every week in the local paper. How could he reduce his costs?

Q3 A firm's cash-flow forecast for the next three months is:

£s	June	July	August
Cash inflow	24,500	36,000	23,500
Cash outflow	22,000	30,000	29,000

The opening bank balance in June was £4,000. What will the closing bank balance be in August?

Answers are on page 158.

Breakeven analysis

⊞ What is the breakeven point?

■ One way of making sure that a cash-flow crisis does not occur is by using breakeven analysis. This shows the **breakeven point**, the level of output at which costs and revenue are exactly the same so that the business makes neither a profit nor a loss. The breakeven point can be shown in a graph, which is known as a breakeven chart (see Figure 4.5).

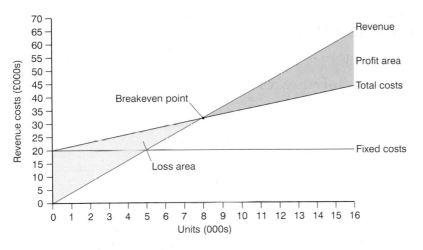

4.5 *Breakeven point*

■ The vertical axis shows the costs and revenue in thousands of pounds. The horizontal axis shows the output in thousands of units.

■ To plot the breakeven point you need to know:

  • the fixed costs, which in this case are £20,000

  • the variable costs, which are £1.50 per unit

  • the selling price, which is £4

■ As you can see in Figure 4.5, the fixed costs of £20,000 are shown as a straight line because they do not vary in the short term.

■ The variable costs of £1.50 per unit increase in relation to output and gradually rise as output increases. They are included in the line on the graph which shows the total costs. As this line includes the fixed costs as well as the variable, it starts at £20,000.

■ The revenue line shows the total value of sales at £4 per unit in thousands of pounds.

■ The breakeven point is where the total costs and revenue lines intersect – at an output of 8,000 units. Below this level of output, the business would be making a loss; above this level of output, the business would be making a profit.

⊞ Calculating the breakeven point

- It is very simple to calculate the breakeven point by using the following formula:

$$\frac{\text{fixed costs}}{\text{selling price} - \text{variable costs}}$$

- This formula can be used with the data in Figure 4.5. The fixed costs are £20,000. The selling price – variable costs is £2.50 (£4 – £1.50). Therefore the breakeven point is 20,000 ÷ 2.5 = 8,000.

- You can use this formula to work out a breakeven point quickly, or to check that the breakeven point on your chart is correct.

⊞ Limitations of breakeven charts

- Breakeven analysis gives a good general view of whether a business will be profitable during the coming year, but it has its limitations. The main ones are:

  - It is only a projection based on a current situation.

  - It does not allow for unexpected rises in fixed costs.

  - Variable costs cannot be accurately estimated because circumstances may change.

  - It does not allow for changes in the selling price.

  - Sales may fall.

  - It does not indicate suitable selling prices.

  - It assumes sales will continue and all stock will be sold.

?

CHECK YOURSELF QUESTIONS

Q1 State two limitations of breakeven charts.

Q2 Calculate the breakeven point when the fixed costs are £15,000 a year, the selling price is £10 and the variable costs are £5, and draw a breakeven chart to illustrate it.

Answers are on page 158.

▦ What are the main internal sources of finance?

■ Businesses need finance for many reasons, including starting the business, modernizing it, beginning new ventures, expansion or support in difficult trading periods. There are two main kinds of finance. **Internal sources of finance** are provided by the business itself. **External sources of finance** are obtained from outside the business.

■ The main internal sources available for all kinds of businesses are:

- profits
- sale of assets
- depreciation

▦ Profits

■ Profits, after tax has been paid, are the main internal source for successful businesses. With sole proprietors, the owner's **drawings** – or money to live on – have to come out of the profits before any surplus profit can be used to improve or expand the business.

DISTRIBUTED PROFIT

■ With companies, profit is divided into two parts. **Distributed profit** is given to the shareholders in the form of **dividends**, an annual or six-monthly payment in return for taking the risk of investing their money. For holders of **ordinary shares**, the dividend will vary from year to year. Holders of the much smaller number of **preference shares** get the same dividend every year.

RETAINED PROFIT

■ **Retained profit** is the money which the business keeps for its own purposes. This is the most important source of finance for business expansion.

▦ Sale of assets

■ A sole proprietor often has to sell a valuable asset, such as a second car or an inherited collection of stamps, to provide funds to start the business. Companies often sell off assets, such as land or subsidiary companies.

■ Selling an asset is a sensible source of finance if it will help the business to expand. But it is a mistake to sell off assets quickly just to raise money, as they often have to be sold at far less than the market price.

⚡ A* EXTRA

Businesses which can fund their own development from internal sources alone retain greater control and have lower risks than businesses which are forced to use external finance from banks or investors.

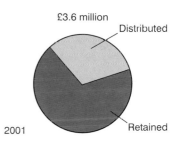

£3.6 million
Distributed
2001
Retained

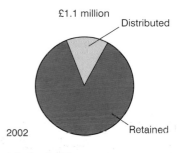

£1.1 million
Distributed
2002
Retained

4.6 *Profit after tax*

⊞ Depreciation

- **Depreciation** is another useful source of finance for all businesses. If a business buys a new car, its value starts to fall immediately it is put on the road, and its value will continue to fall every year after that. For example, a small car which cost £8,000 new might be worth only £6,500 after one year and only £5,000 after two years. This is known as depreciation, or a fall in value over a period of time.

TAX ALLOWANCE

- All businesses receive a tax allowance for the depreciation of fixed assets such as vehicles and machinery. The annual allowance for cars is 25 per cent and currently 100 per cent for IT equipment. This allowance reduces the profits of the business, so that it has to pay less corporation, or business, tax.

ADDITIONAL BENEFIT

- The business also benefits in another way. It has allowed for an expense that it doesn't have to pay immediately. Therefore, it has more cash available to spend on other purposes.

- The amount of depreciation for sole proprietors is often only a few thousand pounds a year, but for big companies, it can be millions.

⊞ Calculating depreciation

- There are two main methods of calculating depreciation.

REDUCING-BALANCE METHOD

- One way is by the **reducing–balance method**. The same percentage of an asset's value is written off, or allowed, for depreciation every year.

- If a car cost £12,000 and the annual depreciation allowance was 25 per cent, the depreciation would be calculated in the following way.

	Value	Depreciation
First year	£12,000	£3,000
Second year	£9,000	£2,250
Third year	£6,750	£1,688
Fourth year	£5,062	£1,266

4.7 *Depreciation (to nearest pound)*

- This method has a high rate of depreciation in the early years, but, as Figure 4.7 shows, it falls rapidly in subsequent years, from £3,000 in the first year to £1,266 in the fourth.

QUESTION SPOTTER

Exam questions might be set on the following:
- What are the two methods of depreciation?
- How does depreciation benefit a business?
- Using the reducing-balance method of depreciation, what would be the total depreciation in the first two years on a new car which cost £17,000?

STRAIGHT-LINE METHOD

■ The second method is **straight-line depreciation**, where the amount of depreciation is the same every year. The firm calculates how long a machine will last and what its residual, or scrap, value will be at the end of its useful life. It then uses the following formula to obtain the annual amount of depreciation:

$$\frac{\text{original cost} - \text{residual value}}{\text{useful life in years}} = \text{annual depreciation}$$

■ For example, a horizontal boring machine cost £20,000 new. Its scrap value after five years will be £5,000. Therefore, the annual straight-line depreciation will be £3,000 (£20,000 – £5,000 = £15,000 ÷ 5 = £3,000).

? CHECK YOURSELF QUESTIONS

Q1 How does a plc use its profits?

Q2 Explain the difference between the reducing-balance and the straight-line methods of depreciation.

Answers are on page 159.

External sources of finance

⊞ What are the main external sources of finance?

- The main external sources that are available for all kinds of businesses are:
  - overdrafts
  - loans
  - hire purchase
  - leasing
  - trade credit
  - grants

- The source that is used depends on:
  - the size of the firm
  - the purpose for which finance is needed
  - the length of time for which the funds are required

⊞ Overdrafts and loans

- An **overdraft** allows a business to withdraw more money from its current bank account than it contains, up to a certain limit agreed previously with the bank manager.

- Most businesses have overdrafts, as they provide funds for periods of negative cash flow, or when there is an unexpected financial emergency. It is a very economical way of borrowing money, as interest is charged on a daily basis only on the amount overdrawn.

- **Bank loans** are one of the main external sources of finance. They are for a fixed amount and for any period of time from one to 20 years, or more.

- Regular repayments of both the capital sum borrowed and of the interest charged have to be made to the bank. This is usually done through a **standing order**, which automatically pays back a fixed amount at regular intervals from the borrower's account.

- Banks also provide businesses with **mortgage loans** to buy property in the same way as a private individual obtains a mortgage to buy a home. The money has to be paid back over a fixed number of years. Insurance companies and building societies also give mortgage loans to businesses.

INTEREST PAYMENTS

- Interest has to be paid on all types of loans. The interest is calculated like any other percentage using the formula:

$$\frac{\text{amount borrowed}}{100} \times \text{percentage rate} = \text{amount of interest}$$

- For example, if you borrowed £1,000 for a year at an interest rate of eight per cent, the interest would be £80 (£1,000 ÷ 100 × 8 = £80). Your total repayment would be £1,080: £1,000 loan and £80 interest.

A* EXTRA

Most businesses have an overdraft facility to cover cash-flow problems or financial emergencies. One big drawback is that a bank can end – or call in – the overdraft at any time. The rate of interest is also variable.

QUESTION SPOTTER

Exam questions might be set on the following:
- ▶ State two kinds of external finance for businesses.
- ▶ A business wants to buy another business. How could the takeover be financed?

NOMINAL RATE OF INTEREST

■ In the above case, eight per cent is the **nominal rate of interest** that is applied to the whole loan from the time it is borrowed until the loan is paid back. Loans are usually paid back in equal instalments, which include both the repayment of the loan and the interest. In this case, the monthly repayment of the amount borrowed and the interest would be £90 a month (£1,080 ÷ 12 = £90).

ANNUAL PERCENTAGE RATE (APR)

■ The nominal rate of interest does not give a true picture of the interest that is actually paid. Each time a monthly repayment is made, some of the original loan is paid off. As the amount of money borrowed is gradually decreasing each month, and the amount of interest paid remains the same, the real rate of interest is actually increasing.

■ The true rate of interest is the **annual percentage rate (APR)**, which is about twice as much as the nominal rate.

DIFFERENT RATES OF INTEREST

■ There are two kinds of interest rates: **fixed** and **variable**. Fixed rates are usually charged for loans, and variable rates for many mortgage loans. The amount of interest charged will depend on a number of factors, including:

- the bank rate, which is determined by the rate of interest set by the Bank of England, the rates charged by banks to each other, and future interest rates

- the degree of risk involved – the likely ability of the borrower to repay and other debts and obligations

- the value of assets offered as security for the loan

- the status of the borrower – big companies can obtain lower interest rates than small businesses

- the amount borrowed and the purpose for which the loan is required

OVERDRAFTS VERSUS LOANS

■ Advantages of overdrafts
  - they are more flexible
  - interest is paid only on the amount that is actually borrowed
  - they usually cost less in interest payments
  - they are useful for covering cash-flow problems

■ Disadvantages of overdrafts
  - they can be called in at any time

■ Advantages of loans
  - they are given for a stated time
  - they are repaid at regular intervals
  - they are suitable for buying assets and expansion

■ Disadvantages of loans
  - they usually cost more in interest payments.

QUESTION SPOTTER

Exam questions might be set on the following:
▶ What are the differences between an overdraft and a bank loan?
▶ Give one example of when a business would use a) an overdraft; b) a short-term loan; c) a long-term loan.

⊞ Hire purchase and leasing

■ **Hire purchase** and **leasing** are other useful sources of finance as they enable businesses to acquire assets such as vehicles and machinery without spending large amounts of cash.

HIRE PURCHASE

■ With hire purchase, the business usually pays the finance house back in monthly instalments (a fixed sum, plus interest). Usually, a deposit has to be paid. The asset does not belong to the business until the last instalment has been paid.

LEASING

■ With leasing, there is usually no deposit and equal repayments at regular intervals, not necessarily monthly. The asset never becomes the property of the business, but at the end of the fixed term, the business receives a proportion of the amount for which the asset is sold.

⊞ Trade credit

■ Businesses do not usually have to pay their suppliers immediately they receive the goods. They have a period of **trade credit**, usually of thirty days, to settle the bill.

⊞ Official grants and loans

■ Various official bodies, including the European Union, the government, local authorities and Training and Enterprise Councils (TECs), provide grants, loans and security guarantees of different kinds for business.

- The European Union provides some grants for firms – and councils – in areas of high unemployment (see Unit 14).

- The government also gives grants to companies, both British and foreign, that create jobs in these same areas by opening new factories.

- The government's Small Firms Loans Guarantee Scheme helps small firms that do not have enough security to obtain a bank loan. It guarantees loans of up to £250,000 for established businesses for up to seven years.

- Some government grants are available through TECs for people who want to start their own business.

- Some local councils also give financial assistance to firms that create new jobs in their area.

⊞ Additional sources of finance

■ Sole proprietors, private limited companies and public limited companies all have some additional sources of finance of their own.

SOLE PROPRIETORS

■ The main extra sources for sole proprietors are:

- **Internal**. The sole proprietor will usually use some of his or her own money to start the business. This now provides a bigger source of start-up capital than bank loans.

- **External.** Friends may be willing to put money into a sole proprietor's business. However, one problem might be that they may try to interfere in the way the business is run, or take their money out suddenly if they need it themselves.

PRIVATE LIMITED COMPANIES

- **Internal.** Established private companies may have some investments in shares that they can sell to finance their core business or to finance expansion.

- **External.** There are several external sources of finance available to private limited companies:

  - **Venture capital.** Small companies with big ideas may find it difficult to obtain finance from banks. They can sometimes obtain venture, or risk, capital from other financial organizations and groups of rich people who invest in companies with good ideas.

  - **Selling shares.** Although a private company cannot sell shares to members of the public, it can sell them to business associates or friends.

  - **Going public.** The amount of money that can be raised from friends or business associates is limited. If a medium-sized company wants to raise greater amounts of money for expansion, it could go public, or become a public limited company (plc). However, it is very expensive to set up a public limited company.

PUBLIC LIMITED COMPANIES

- **Internal sources**

  - **Sale of subsidiary companies.** Public limited companies often have subsidiary companies. They can sell these to raise money for expansion so that they can concentrate more on their core business.

  - **Sale and leaseback.** Plcs can raise additional money by selling their own headquarters (or other buildings) which they own. They sell it to a property company or developer and then lease it back for an agreed number of years. In this way, they obtain the finance they want, but still keep the use of their headquarters for a number of years.

- **External sources**

  - **Selling shares.** The main external source of finance for plcs is selling **ordinary shares**. A company can issue shares up to the limit of its nominal, or authorized, capital, which is stated in its memorandum of association. A plc, however, does not issue all its shares when it is formed, but keeps some in reserve to be sold later.

  - The main advantage of selling shares is that the money raised never has to be repaid. It belongs to the company.

  - **Debentures.** Money is lent to a plc for a fixed period of time at a fixed rate of interest. At the end of that period, the money must be repaid. The terms of the loan are set out in a document called a debenture. The interest on the debenture has to be paid, even if the firm does not make a profit.

A* EXTRA

One disadvantage of using venture capital is that the owners of the business often have to sacrifice some of their independence by making the venture capitalist a director.

QUESTION SPOTTER

Exam questions might be set on the following:
▸ State one internal and one external source of finance for a) a private limited company and b) a public limited company.
▸ What is the main external source of finance for a plc?
▸ When might a plc sell a subsidiary company?

• **Factoring.** Plcs with large amounts of debts can employ a factor to collect them. The factor pays the firm immediately for about three-quarters of the debts. When all the debts have been collected, the factor pays the firm the balance, less the charges for its services.

⊞ Long-term and short-term sources of finance

■ External sources of finance can be divided into short term and long term.

Short term	Long term
Overdrafts	Mortgage loans
Short-term bank loan (up to two years)	Long-term bank loan (up to twenty years)
Hire purchase	Government and other official assistance
Factoring	Venture capital
Trade credit	Share capital
	Debentures

Leasing may be either short term, for vehicles or equipment, or long term for property. Friends' loans for sole proprietors may also be either short term or long term.

4.8 *Long-term and short-term sources of finance*

? CHECK YOURSELF QUESTIONS

Q1 How long does trade credit usually last?

Q2 Describe the main differences between hire purchase and leasing.

Q3 Mustapha Bagheri owns a small, but very successful, export/import company, whose profits have doubled in each of the last two years. As a result, he has more than £240,000 in a deposit account at the bank. Mustapha has decided to equip his sales force of three with new cars, which will cost £14,500 each.

a What would be the total cost of the cars?

b If he bought them on hire purchase over two years at an interest rate of 12 per cent, what would be the total cost?

c Would you advise him to buy the cars on hire purchase or pay cash? State your reasons.

Answers are on page 159.

UNIT 5: ACCOUNTS

Business accounts

⊞ Why do businesses keep accounts?

■ All businesses have to keep **accounts**, or financial records, of their business transactions every day. Everything is recorded, from buying a postage stamp to buying a new headquarters.

WHAT ACCOUNTS CONTAIN

■ The accounts provide:

- • a complete record of the business's recent financial history

- • an up-to-date description of its present financial situation

- • an indication of what is likely to happen in the future

■ For these reasons alone a business would need to keep accounts, but it is also forced to keep records – and retain them for six years – by law.

DIFFERENCE BETWEEN SOLE PROPRIETOR AND COMPANY ACCOUNTS

■ Sole proprietors are obliged to show their accounts only to the Inland Revenue, which collects taxes, and to the Customs and Excise, if they are liable to pay duties or VAT. Companies, on the other hand, have to send a copy of their annual accounts to the Registrar of Companies and to all their shareholders.

⊞ Annual report and accounts

■ Many companies have realized that the **annual report and accounts** says a lot about themselves and their attitudes. They have brightened up their documents so that some of them now look like glossy magazines.

⊞ Who is interested in these accounts?

■ Shareholders are interested in the accounts of companies in which they hold shares. There are now about 15 million shareholders in the UK. Some of them bought shares when industries were privatised in the 1980s and 1990s. Millions more became shareholders in the late 1990s when building societies such as the Halifax and Alliance and Leicester converted to banks and gave shares to all their borrowers and savers.

■ The other people and organizations interested in company accounts include:

- • investors and speculators who are thinking of buying shares in the company

- • banks, suppliers and other creditors who want to make sure that the company is in a healthy financial state so that it will be able to pay its bills

---

💡 QUESTION SPOTTER

Exam questions might be set on the following:

▸ State two reasons why businesses keep financial accounts.

▸ The number of shareholders in Britain has increased in the last 20 years. Explain why this might be.

▸ Explain why a trade union would be interested in the accounts of any large corporation which employed a large number of its members.

- employees and trade unions who want to obtain financial information to support their claim for a pay rise

- other companies in the same line of business that want to make comparisons with their own results

- other companies that are thinking of making a takeover bid

- financial journalists and City analysts who have to recommend whether a company's shares should be bought or not

■ The managers of the firm will also be interested in the accounts. However, they have access to much more detailed information, which is contained in the firm's budget. This is not available to the public.

▦ Who compiles the accounts?

FINANCIAL ACCOUNTANTS

■ The accounts are put together by **financial accountants**. Their main job is to make sure that the accounts are a 'true and fair' record of the business's financial transactions.

AUDITORS

■ To make sure that the accounts are accurate, plc accounts have to be checked by an independent **auditor**.

MANAGEMENT ACCOUNTANTS

■ Big companies also employ **management accountants**, who are more concerned with the present and the future rather than recording what has happened in the past.

▦ Principles of accounting

■ There are four main principles and conventions by which all accountants operate.

- **Prudence and caution**. Accountants take a prudent (or sensible and careful) view of finance, so that they undervalue future revenue or profits rather than exaggerating them.

- **Consistency**. They always use the same methods of valuing assets, or of allocating costs.

- **Materiality**. They record all transactions which are material (or important) to the business concerned. For example, they would record that a sole proprietor had spent £800 on stationery in a year if it was a substantial part of his or her costs, but with a company it would be included under 'office administration', along with many other items.

- **Matching**. All costs and revenue are included in the accounts for the year in which they occur. Bills for services rendered during the year are included in costs, even though they have not been paid.

⚡ A* EXTRA

▸ An auditor does not have to check every small detail in a firm's accounts. She or he has to make sure only that they give a true and fair view of the company's financial situation.

▸ Financial accountants look after a company's financial records; management accountants prepare annual budgets and longer-term forecasts, and assess the financial consequences of a company's plans.

FINAL ACCOUNTS

- Every year, a business prepares final accounts, which give a summary of all the financial transactions that have occurred during the financial year.

- The three main final accounts are:

  1 the trading account

  2 the profit and loss account

  3 the balance sheet

CHECK YOURSELF QUESTIONS

Q1 Using the words below, complete the following statements about accounts.

balance sheet   management   accountants
auditors   consistency

  a ____ prepare long-term financial plans.

  b The ____ is one of the final accounts.

  c Company accounts are checked by ____ to make sure that they give a true and fair view of its financial affairs.

  d One of the four principles of accounting is ____ .

Q2 State two organizations that might be interested in reading companies' final accounts.

Q3 Why do firms keep accounts?

Answers are on page 160.

■ Trading accounts ■

⊞ What is a trading account?

■ The **trading account** shows the difference between a firm's sales, or its **turnover**, and the **cost of sales**, or what it cost the firms to buy (or make) the goods.

■ For example, Don, who owns a small bicycle shop, might spend £90,000 on buying goods during the year and have a turnover, or total sales, of £120,000.

■ In a summary of a trading account, this might be recorded as:

Trading account	
	£
Sales	120,000
Cost of sales	90,000
Gross profit	30,000

■ The difference between the sales and cost of sales is the **gross profit**. In this case, it is £30,000.

⊞ Changes in stock values

■ The summary above does not give a complete picture of what has happened during the year, as it omits the different values of the stock, or goods available for sale, at the beginning and the end of the year.

■ You will sometimes come across a full trading account, like the one in Figure 5.1 below, which includes the value of stock at the beginning and the end of the financial year.

	£	£	£
Sales			120,000
Opening stock	30,000		
Purchases	80,000		
less closing stock	20,000		
Cost of sales		90,000	
Gross profit		30,000	
		120,000	120,000

5.1 *A full trading account*

■ To make sure that you understand the trading account, let's go through it line by line.

• **Sales:** This is the firm's revenue, or the total value of its sales, during the year.

• **Opening stock:** The left-hand column is used to calculate the effects of changes in stock value during the year. This line gives the stock value at the beginning of the financial year.

- **Purchases:** This line shows the value of all the goods purchased for sale during the year.

- **less closing stock:** This is the value of the stock at the end of the financial year. To calculate the cost of sales, the opening stock and purchases are added together to give £110,000 (£30,000 + £80,000 = £110,000). The value of the closing stock is then subtracted to give £90,000 (£110,000 – £20,000 = £90,000).

- **Cost of sales:** After allowance has been made for the changes in stock value, the actual cost of sales to the business (what it has paid for the goods) is £90,000.
  Note that this is recorded in the second column of the account, which is one of the two main columns.

- **Gross profit:** The cost of sales (£90,000) is deducted from the sales (£120,000) in the right-hand column, the other main column of the accounts. The gross profit, therefore, is £30,000 (£120,000 – £90,000 = £30,000).

Exam questions might be set on the following:
- ▸ What is another name for 'total sales'?
- ▸ Explain the term 'cost of sales'.
- ▸ How do you calculate gross profit?

DOUBLE-ENTRY METHOD

- Note that the totals in the main columns (the second and third) are equal. This is because accounts are based on the **double-entry method**. Transactions are recorded as **debits**, or debts, on the left-hand side of the accounts. **Credits**, or payments received, are recorded on the right-hand side.

VERTICAL FORMAT

- The accounts of most big companies, however, are now recorded in a vertical format with one item under another, as in Figure 5.2. The basic information it contains is still the same, though many of the details are given in a separate set of notes at the end of the accounts.

Consolidated profit and loss account
52 weeks ended 31 March 2001

	Notes	Before exceptional items £m	Exceptional items £m	After exceptional items £m
Turnover	2	8,075.7	-	8,075.7
Cost of sales		(5,237.2)	-	(5,237.2)
Gross profit		2,838.5	-	2,838.5
Net operating expenses	3,4A	(2,371.5)	(26.5)	(2,398.0)
Operating profit	2	467.0	(26.5)	440.5
Loss on sale of property and other fixed assets	4B	-	(83.2)	(83.2)
Loss on sale/termination of operations	4C	-	(1.7)	(1.7)
Provision for loss on operations to be discontinued	4D	-	(224.0)	(224.0)
Net interest income	5	13.9	-	13.9
Profit on ordinary activities before taxation		480.9	(335.4)	145.5
Taxation on ordinary activities	6	(151.2)	8.5	(142.7)
Profit on ordinary activities after taxation		329.7	(326.9)	2.8
Minority interests (all equity)		(1.5)	-	(1.5)
Profit attributable to shareholders	7	328.2	(326.9)	1.3
Dividends	8	(258.3)		(258.3)
Retained profit/(loss) for the period		69.9	(326.9)	(257.0)
Basic earnings per share	9	0.0p		
Diluted basic earnings per share	9	0.0p		
Adjusted earnings per share	9	11.4p		
Diluted adjusted earnings per share	9	11.4p		
Dividend per share	8	9.0p		

5.2 *A profit-and-loss account in vertical format*
Source: Marks and Spencer plc

⊞ Finding ratios from the trading account

- A ratio is the relationship between two quantities, e.g. the gross profit and sales. The result is usually expressed as a percentage, or in numbers, e.g. 2:1.

- Ratios make it possible to compare a business's results with those of similar businesses, even if they are much bigger. They are also used for comparing a business's results in the current year with those in previous years.

GROSS PROFIT MARGIN

- One important ratio which can be calculated from the trading account is the gross profit margin, or gross profit-to-sales ratio. This shows what percentage of sales is gross profit.

- The formula for calculating the ratio is:

$$\frac{\text{gross profit}}{\text{sales}} \times 100 = \text{gross profit margin}$$

- Using this formula, the gross profit margin of Don's shop would be:

$$\frac{£30,000}{£120,000} \times 100 = 25\%$$

- This ratio can then be compared with ratios of other retailers.

STOCK TURNOVER RATIO

- Another useful ratio which can be obtained from the trading account is the rate of stock turnover. The formula for the stock turnover ratio is:

$$\frac{\text{cost of sales}}{\text{average stock}} = \text{rate of stock turnover}$$

- To calculate average stock, you have to calculate the average value of stock held during the year. This is found by the formula:

$$\frac{\text{stock at start of year} + \text{stock at end of year}}{2} = \text{average stock}$$

- Don's stock at the beginning of the year was £30,000 and at the end, £20,000. Therefore, his average stock was £25,000:

$$\frac{£30,000 + £20,000}{2} = £25,000$$

- You can now calculate the stock turnover rate. The cost of sales was £90,000 and the average stock was £25,000. Therefore the rate of stock turnover was 3.6 times:

$$\frac{£90,000}{£25,000} = 3.6 \text{ times}$$

⊞ Analysis of the stock turnover ratio

■ The stock turnover rate is one guide to the efficiency of the business. The more often the stock is turned over, the greater the profit will be.

■ However, not all kinds of business turn over stock at the same rate. Food shops selling fast-moving consumer goods turn over stock at a high rate and can therefore afford to take a smaller profit on each item. An antique shop, on the other hand, sells very few items in comparison with a food shop. It therefore has a much lower stock turnover rate and needs to make a much bigger profit on each item.

■ Don's rate of stock turnover is quite reasonable for his type of business. As his gross profit is comparatively low, it seems that he needs to put up his prices or find cheaper suppliers so that he can make a higher profit.

CHECK YOURSELF QUESTIONS

Q1 Explain why businesses need to find out their gross profit margin.

Q2 a Fill in the missing numbers in the trading account below:

	£	£
Sales		200,000
Opening stock	80,000	
Purchases	120,000	
less closing stock	90,000	
Cost of sales		
Gross profit		

b What was the gross profit margin?

Q3 a A business's cost of sales during the year was £365,000 and the average stock was £81,000. What was the rate of stock turnover?

b A firm's stock at the beginning of the year was worth £42,000. At the end of the year, the value of the stock was £58,000. During the year, it bought £150,000 worth of goods. What was its stock turnover rate?

Answers are on page 160.

Profit and loss accounts

What is net profit?

- The second of the final accounts is the **profit and loss account**, which shows how much **net profit** (or loss) a business has made during the previous year. The net profit (or operating profit) is the amount that remains after all the expenses of running the business, or overheads, have been subtracted from the gross profit.

- The net profit is always much smaller than the gross profit.

A sample profit and loss account

- Sarah owns a small boutique. Her profit and loss account is shown here:

£		
Gross profit		90,000
Rent, rates, insurance	15,800	
Wages	18,000	
Lighting and heating	4,700	
Office expenses	2,250	
Advertising	3,500	
Telephone	900	
Total overheads	45,150	
Net profit	44,850	
	90,000	90,000

5.3 *Sarah's profit and loss account*

- The overheads in the left-hand column total £45,150. This has to be subtracted from the gross profit of £90,000 to give a net profit of £44,850 (£90,000 − £45,150 = £44,850).

OTHER ITEMS

- There could also have been other overheads, such as interest on any loans, which would have been included in the left-hand column. Any depreciation (see Unit 4) would also have been included.

- If Sarah had any other income from the business, such as interest on a deposit account, this would have been included in the right-hand side of the account.

TAX AND DRAWINGS

- Sarah would have paid tax on the net profit. Her drawings, or the amount of money she needed to live on, would have come out of the profit that remained after tax had been paid.

Net profit to sales ratio

- Sarah's turnover during the year was £300,000. Another useful ratio can be calculated from these figures, the net profit to sales ratio, or **net profit margin**.

- The formula is:

$$\frac{\text{net profit}}{\text{sales}} \times 100 = \text{net profit margin}$$

- In this case, it would be nearly 15 per cent:

$$\frac{£44,850}{£300,000} \times 100 = 14.95\%$$

- This provides a better indication of a business's performance than the gross profit margin, as the amount of profit that remains when all overheads have been paid is what really counts.

Consolidated profit and loss accounts

- In the annual accounts of plcs and other big companies, the trading account and the profit and loss account are usually consolidated, or combined. The first part of a plc's consolidated profit and loss account might read:

	£000
Turnover	15,360
Cost of sales	(12,560)
Gross profit	2,800
Operating expenses	(1,962)
Operating profit	838

- There are certain points you should note about this account:

  - The term **'operating profit'** is used instead of 'net profit'.

  - Brackets are used to indicate negative amounts.

  - The account is in a vertical format, with numbers under each other and not in separate columns, as in smaller business' accounts.

  - The combined total is given for some items, such as operating expenses.

5.4 *Part of a consolidated profit and loss account*

QUESTION SPOTTER

In your exam you might be asked to:
- do simple calculations to find costs of sales or overheads.
- calculate ratios.
- explain why one company is more financially successful than another by examining its accounts.

CHECK YOURSELF QUESTIONS

Q1 What is operating profit?

Q2 Give three examples of overheads which might be included in a profit and loss account.

Q3 Look at Figure 5.4.

  a How much is the net profit?

  b Calculate the gross profit margin.

  c How would you use this ratio to judge the performance of the company?

Answers are on page 161.

Balance sheets

QUESTION SPOTTER

Exam questions might be set on the following:
▸ Give one example of a tangible asset.
▸ What is the difference between a fixed asset and a tangible asset?
▸ Why is it necessary for a business to produce a balance sheet?

▦ What is a balance sheet?

■ The last of the three final accounts is the **balance sheet**. This gives a picture of the financial situation of a business at one moment in time – the end of the financial year. It shows what the business owns – its **assets** – and what the company owes – its **liabilities**.

A sample balance sheet

■ Let's look at the first part of a balance sheet of a fictional manufacturing company – Eastern Engineering plc.

	£000
Fixed assets	
Tangible assets	12,000
Investments	300
	12,300
Current assets	
Stock	1,600
Debtors	11,800
Cash at bank or in hand	400
	13,800
Creditors	
amounts falling due within one year	(12,100)
Net current assets	1,700
Total assets less current liabilities	14,000
Creditors: amounts falling due after one year	(4,500)
	9,500

5.5 *Eastern Engineering plc's balance sheet (part 1)*

▦ Analysing the balance sheet

■ To help you understand the balance sheet and all the important key terms associated with it, let's go through it line by line.

■ Note that all the numbers are given in thousands, as in the other company's profit and loss account in Figure 5.4, so that you have to add 000 to each figure to obtain the true number.

FIXED ASSETS
■ Some of the assets, or items which are owned by the company, are actually fixed, such as land or buildings. However, accountants use the term '**fixed assets**' in a different sense to mean assets that will stay in the business for at least a year.

TANGIBLE ASSETS
■ **Tangible assets** are physical assets, such as land, buildings, machinery, vehicles and fixtures and fittings.

INVESTMENTS

■ Investments are non-physical fixed assets. The tangible assets and investments are added to give the total value of fixed assets: £12,000,000 + £300,000 = £12,300,000.

CURRENT ASSETS

■ In contrast to fixed assets, the **current assets** change in value from day to day as stock is sold and bills are paid.

STOCK

■ **Stock** is one of the main elements in a business's current assets. With manufacturing companies, stock includes raw materials, work in progress and finished goods. With retailers, stock is the goods that the business has for sale.

DEBTORS

■ **Debtors** are people or organizations that owe money to the company. Most of it is usually owed by other firms who have been given credit.

CASH AT BANK OR IN HAND

■ This shows the total of cash in the current account at the bank, plus the cash on the premises. The three items – stock, debtors and cash at bank or in hand – are added to give the total value of current assets: £1,600,000 + £11,800,000 + £400,000 = £13,800,000.

CREDITORS: AMOUNTS FALLING DUE WITHIN ONE YEAR

■ This shows the amount of money the company owes which will have to be paid within a year, or the **current liabilities**. It includes **trade creditors**, to whom the company owes money, bank overdrafts and **provisions** for tax bills and payment of dividends to shareholders. (Provisions are allowances made for current liabilities which a business knows it will have to pay within the year.)

NET CURRENT ASSETS

■ The net current assets are calculated by deducting the current liabilities from the total of current assets in the section above, i.e. £13,800,000 – £12,100,000 = £1,700,000.

■ This is the **working capital**, a most important key term that you must remember and know how to calculate, because it comes up in so many exam papers. The working capital shows the total amount of short-term capital a business has available to meet its day-by-day cash requirements. If it fell too low, the business would have a cash-flow problem.

■ Remember the formula:

> current assets – current liabilities = working capital

TOTAL ASSETS LESS CURRENT LIABILITIES

■ These numbers are found by adding the fixed assets to the net current assets, i.e. £12,300,000 + £1,700,000 = £14,000,000. The current liabilities have already been allowed for in the calculation of the net current assets.

Exam questions might be set on the following:
▸ Give one example of a) a debtor; b) a creditor.
▸ What amount is found by deducting current liabilities from current assets?
▸ What kind of problem would a business have if this amount was negative or very low? If it was a negative figure, what action could the business take?

CREDITORS: AMOUNTS FALLING DUE AFTER ONE YEAR

■ Finally, the company's debts, which are due to be repaid after more than one year, are deducted from the total assets. They could include bank loans, mortgages and debentures.

■ The final line shows what the company is worth after all debts and loans have been repaid: £9,500,000.

⊞ Capital and reserves

■ The second part of the balance sheet shows the shareholders' funds. These consist of the capital, or the amount of money that the owners have put into the business, and the capital reserves, or the extra value of assets that have been revalued mainly because of inflation.

■ Eastern Engineering's capital and reserves are shown in Figure 5.6. We'll also look at this part of the balance sheet line by line.

Capital and reserves	
	£000
Called-up share capital	2,050
Share premium account	4,400
Revaluation reserve	650
Profit and loss account	2,400
Shareholders' funds	9,500

5.6 *Eastern Engineering plc's balance sheet (part 2)*

CALLED-UP SHARE CAPITAL

■ This shows the nominal, or stated, value of the shares that the company has sold. They were sold at this price when the company started.

SHARE PREMIUM ACCOUNT

■ Shares that were issued later, when the company was running successfully, were sold at a premium, or higher, price. This extra money has gone into the share premium account.

REVALUATION RESERVE

■ This is the amount by which the company's fixed assets have been revalued because of inflation.

PROFIT AND LOSS ACCOUNT

■ This line shows the surpluses transferred from the profit and loss account over the years.

SHAREHOLDERS' FUNDS

■ The final line shows the shareholders' funds, or the company's total liability to its shareholders – £9,500,000. Note that it balances exactly with the assets, which are shown in the first part of the balance sheet (Figure 5.5).

■ In a smaller firm's accounts, the liabilities would be shown on the left-hand side and the assets on the right. The totals would be exactly the same so that the accounts balanced.

⚡ A* EXTRA

The amount of shareholders' funds is an important figure in financial management, as it is used to calculate one of the most important ratios, ROCE, or return on capital employed.

CHECK YOURSELF QUESTIONS

Q1 State which of the following terms are assets and which are liabilities:

stock

bank loan

creditors

capital

cash at bank

Q2 Explain the term 'fixed assets' and give two examples.

Q3 a In which final account would you find a business's working capital?

b How would you calculate it?

c Why is it important for the business?

Answers are on page 162.

Balance sheet ratios

5.7 *Eastern Engineering plc's balance sheet (part 3)*

⊞ Current ratio

- Some important ratios are calculated from the balance sheet. One of the most important – and a favourite exam question – is the **current ratio**, or **working capital ratio**.

- This is an indicator of the firm's liquidity (see Unit 4), or whether it has enough money to pay its debts. To calculate this ratio, you need to know a business's current assets and current liabilities.

- The relevant part of Eastern Engineering plc's balance sheet is shown in Figure 5.7.

	£000
Current assets	
Stock	1,600
Debtors	11,800
Cash at bank or in hand	400
	13,800
Creditors	
amounts falling due within one year	(12,100)

- The current ratio is calculated by the following formula:

$$\frac{\text{current assets}}{\text{current liabilities}} = \text{current ratio}$$

- Therefore, Eastern Engineering's current ratio would be:

$$\frac{£13,800,000}{£12,100,000} = 1.14$$

- This is expressed as 1.14:1, or sometimes as just 1.14.

- This shows that Eastern Engineering has more than enough current assets to meet all its current liabilities, with some to spare.

⊞ Comparing current ratios

- Businesses can compare their working capital ratio with other successful businesses in the same sector to see whether it is too high or low. They can also compare their present year's ratio with last year's.

- For example, with Eastern Engineering, the present and past year's current assets and liabilities, shown in Figure 5.8, were:

	£000	
	2002	2001
Current assets		
Stock	1,600	2,100
Debtors	11,800	10,100
Cash at bank or in hand	400	500
	13,800	12,700
Creditors:		
amounts falling due within one year	(12,100)	(10,150)

5.8 Eastern Engineering plc's assets and liabilities

- The current ratio for the previous year was 1.25 (£12,700,000 ÷ £10,150,000 = 1.25).

INTERPRETING CURRENT RATIOS

- This is a higher figure than the present year's ratio of 1.14, which means that it had greater cover for its current liabilities. As a result, it would have had less chance of any cash-flow problem. However, it does not mean that the business was performing better.

- If you look at Figure 5.8, you will see that the level of stock has been significantly reduced in the current year and that there is a greater volume of both debtors and creditors. This means that the business is doing more trade and selling more of its goods, so that the profit will be greater.

⊞ Acid test ratio

- You may come across the acid test ratio in some exam papers. It provides an even stricter test of a business's liquidity. Stocks, which cannot necessarily be sold quickly, are omitted from the calculations.

- This ratio shows whether the company would be able to meet its current liabilities without being forced to sell its stock. The formula is:

$$\frac{\text{current assets} - \text{stocks}}{\text{current liabilities}} = \text{acid test ratio}$$

- In the case of Eastern Engineering, the current assets minus stocks for 2002 are £12,200,000 (£13,800,000 − £1,600,000 = £12,200,000) and the current liabilities are £12,100,000. The acid test ratio is therefore 1:1 (£12,200,000 ÷ £12,100,000 = 1.00). This means that the company could meet all its current liabilities without being forced to sell its stock quickly, probably at a great loss

> ### ⚡ A * EXTRA
>
> Although the acid test ratio still crops up in exam papers, real-life companies are willing to work with a negative ratio, so long as they have a healthy cash flow. This enables them to use their assets more efficiently.

⊞ Return on capital employed ratio

■ The **return on capital employed ratio (ROCE)** is one of the most important ratios as it shows how efficiently the company is using its capital to produce profit. Numbers from both the balance sheet and the profit and loss account are needed to calculate this ratio.

■ The formula is:

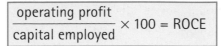

$$\frac{\text{operating profit}}{\text{capital employed}} \times 100 = \text{ROCE}$$

■ Let's say that Eastern Engineering's operating profit in the current year was £1,625,000. We know that the capital employed was £9,500,000. Therefore, its ROCE was 17.1 per cent (£1,625,000 ÷ £9,500,000 × 100 = 17.1%).

■ The ROCE is a much better guide to the efficiency of a company than the net profit margin. The latter shows what percentage profit has been made, but the former, the ROCE, shows how much profit has been made in relation to the resources employed. The higher the ROCE, the more efficiently a company is performing.

CHECK YOURSELF QUESTIONS

Q1 The current assets and liabilities of a company are:

£000	2000	1999
Current assets	120	110
Current liabilities	104	98

What is the working capital ratio for each year?

Q2 A plc – Company X – has a turnover of £12 million, an operating profit of £2,500,000 and capital employed of £20 million.

A smaller private company in the same sector – Company Y – has a turnover of £4,500,000, an operating profit of £800,000 and capital employed of £4 million.

a Explain which company is more profitable.

b State which company is performing most efficiently, giving reasons.

Answers are on page 162.

UNIT 6: FINDING A MARKET

Different markets

⊞ Kinds of market

- Markets are the basis of all modern business. If a business is to survive, it can no longer afford to be only product-orientated and concentrate mainly on its products and their quality. It must also market its products, by studying the people or organizations who might buy its goods or services, and ensure that its products are what they want to buy.

- Most modern markets are highly specialized. They deal almost entirely in new goods, or services.

- There are four main kinds of market.

COMMODITY MARKETS

- **Commodity markets** deal in primary sector raw materials, for example metals and foodstuffs, such as wheat. Unlike the three other kinds of market, commodity markets are almost entirely product oriented. Both buyers and sellers are more interested in the quality of the goods than anything else.

commodity

INDUSTRIAL OR ORGANIZATIONAL MARKETS

- **Industrial markets** or **organizational markets** deal in the vast range of goods and services which other businesses need in order to function efficiently. These include capital goods such as machine tools, used by manufacturers to make their own goods, and security services for government offices. Some of the goods, such as cars and computers, are also sold in consumer markets.

industrial/organizational

- Until recently, these markets were also mainly product oriented. Increasingly, however, they are becoming more market oriented.

- Machine-tool manufacturers often question industrial customers about their needs and ask them to test prototypes.

FINANCIAL MARKETS

- **Financial markets** are one of the fastest-growing in the modern world, where top employees pocket annual salaries of millions of pounds.

financial

- The services that banks and other financial institutions provide have long been divided into separate sections for personal and business customers. Increasingly, the services for personal customers have become more market oriented.

CONSUMER MARKETS

- Much activity in the other three markets helps the production of goods and services for the **consumer market**, which is the most important in the whole economy. It is also the most market oriented.

consumer

6.1 Types of market

QUESTION SPOTTER

Exam questions might be set on the following:

▸ Give one example of
  a) a commodity market;
  b) an industrial market;
  c) a financial market;
  d) a consumer market.
▸ What is the difference between product-oriented goods and market-oriented goods?
▸ Why have industrial markets become more market oriented?

Different market segments

- There is not just one consumer market, but literally many thousands, as a quick glance through any copy of Yellow Pages will show.

- Each market is also split up into many different market segments. Take clothes as an example. There are hundreds of different kinds of clothes. Manufacturers do not try to make clothes for all types of consumers. Instead, they decide whether they are going to specialize in men's, women's or children's clothes, luxury clothes for a few, or mass-market clothes for millions.

- Clothes retailers also specialize. Shops and stores stock the kinds of clothes that will appeal to their chosen market segments – subgroups of customers with similar tastes and wants. Sub-groups in a women's fashion segment, for example, might be smart casual, quality classic, brand lover, career mover.

What unites members of market segments?

- Consumers in the same market segment have similar wants and tastes because they are like each other in a number of ways. One of the most important characteristics is the **socio-economic group** to which they belong.

SOCIO-ECONOMIC GROUPS

- Consumers are divided into six socio-economic groups, or social grades, which are based on the occupation, or job, of the head of the household. These groups are important as they give some idea of size of the household's income and how it might be spent. The six groups are shown below.

A* EXTRA

A new social class structure of eight groups was used for the national census in 2001. Other market researchers now use other categories, such as lifestyle, to segment consumers.

Group	Job description	Examples
A	Higher managerial, administrative, professional	Chief executive, senior civil servant, surgeon
B	Intermediate managerial, administrative, professional	Bank manager, teacher
C1	Supervisory, clerical, junior managerial	Shopfloor supervisor, bank clerk, salesperson
C2	Skilled manual workers	Electrician, carpenter
D	Semi-skilled and unskilled manual workers	Assembly-line worker, refuse collector, messenger
E	Casual labourers, pensioners, unemployed	Pensioners without private pensions, anyone living on basic state benefits

6.2 Socio-economic groups

OTHER FACTORS IN MARKET SEGMENTATION

■ In addition, there are many other characteristics which members of the same market segment may share. The most important are:

- **Age**: very important, as members of the same age group usually have many similar wants.

- **Gender, or sex**: still very important but becoming a little less so, with an increasing number of unisex products appealing to both men and women.

- **Size and composition of household**: the number of adults and children in the household has a big effect on the quantity and kinds of goods and services that are bought.

- **Geographical location**: less important, as people in all parts of the country increasingly have similar wants.

- **Ethnic groups**: of growing importance in a multicultural society.

- **Religion**: now has much less effect than it did.

- **Education**: there are now many more educated consumers because of the growth in higher education.

⊞ Niche markets

■ Sometimes, a business will spot a gap in the market which no other firm has seen. It may be a small group of people who share a great enthusiasm for a special kind of product, like sports cars. These **niche markets**, which are part of a larger market segment, are often small, but they can be highly profitable.

■ Niche markets are particularly suitable for small businesses, as they can afford to devote the time and attention to them which would be unprofitable for a big firm. The number of niche markets has greatly increased because there are many more people who can afford to indulge in minority hobbies and lifestyles. If a niche market attracts more and more customers, it can eventually become a main segment.

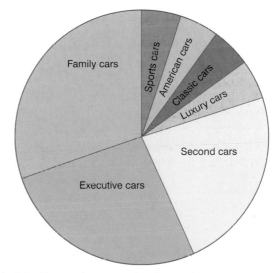

6.3 *Main segments and niche markets*

⊞ Market segmentation in services

■ There is also market segmentation in services as well as goods. Often, different kinds of services are provided for various segments at the same time.

■ Take airlines as an example. They provide the same basic service for all passengers by flying them from one airport to another, but they treat each segment very differently. There is a first class for the most wealthy passengers, club class mainly for business travellers and economy class for all other passengers.

⊞ Benefits of segmentation

■ Market segmentation has many advantages. It enables businesses to:

- increase market share by satisfying more of their customers' wants

- tailor their products so that they will have a greater appeal for their chosen market segments

- become aware of changes and trends in their own segment more quickly

- focus their marketing campaigns and advertising more accurately

- raise profits by increasing sales

CHECK YOURSELF QUESTIONS

Q1 What are the four main kinds of markets?

Q2 Explain two advantages of market segmentation.

Q3 What is a niche market? Give one example.

Answers are on page 163.

▦ Purposes of market research

■ **Market research** is the main way of finding data, or information, that will help a business to find out what consumers want – or may want in the future. Some of the main purposes are to:

- obtain detailed information about a market

- identify potential customers who might buy the product

- test a product which a business plans to produce by giving consumers information about it or by providing a sample

- find out what customers want, why they prefer one product to another, what makes them buy and what they are prepared to pay

- compare the business's performance with that of its rivals

- plan an advertising campaign and to assess its results

- help solve specific problems such as the reasons for a decline in sales

▦ Methods of market research

■ There are two main methods of market research:

1 **Primary research**, or **field research**, obtains original data or information which did not exist before.

2 **Desk research**, or **secondary research**, uses data or information which already exists in printed form or in computer files.

▦ What is desk research?

■ There are two main types of secondary research: external and internal.

EXTERNAL DESK RESEARCH
■ Some of the main sources are:

- Official business information, including a vast quantity and range of information from the European Union, government departments, local councils and other public bodies.

- Unofficial business information, including business directories, such as *Who Owns Whom?* and the Yellow Pages.

- Trade associations and trade magazines.

INTERNAL DESK RESEARCH
■ A business's own accounts, reports and research papers provide extensive details about its own markets.

QUESTION SPOTTER

Exam questions might be set on the following:

▸ Give one difference between primary and secondary research.

▸ What are the advantages and disadvantages of desk research?

▸ Explain why an exporter might use desk research to investigate a new foreign market.

A* EXTRA

Primary data is usually obtained by a quota sample survey, in which a representative sample of the total population is asked the same questions from a structured questionnaire.

ADVANTAGES AND DISADVANTAGES OF DESK RESEARCH

■ Desk, or secondary, research is much easier and cheaper than field research, because the data are already available and do not have to be collected and analysed. However, it is less valuable because it is often out of date and does not always cover the specific subject of enquiry.

RESEARCHING FOREIGN MARKETS

■ External desk research is also useful for making initial investigations of foreign markets to see if they would be suitable for exports. It can provide data on the market size, differences in lifestyles and spending patterns, local incomes, competitors' prices and much other data.

What is field research?

■ Field research, or primary research, involves collecting original data or information from a variety of people and organizations.

ADVANTAGES AND DISADVANTAGES

■ The primary data obtained by field research are very valuable, because they are not available to any other businesses, unless they do their own research. When the information has been obtained, it has to be collated, or put together, and then analysed before a report can be produced.

METHODS OF OBTAINING PRIMARY DATA

■ Primary data are collected in a number of ways. The most important are:

- **Face-to-face interviews**: Interviewers, using printed questionnaires, interview people in the street, on the doorstep, in their home or at their workplace. This method – **a consumer survey** – is the oldest form of field research and still the most common.

- **Telephone interviews**: These are now used more frequently.

- **Postal questionnaires**: These are now more popular than telephone interviews.

- **Focus groups**: A small group of people are brought together and asked to express their opinions and their feelings about products and wider issues. Sometimes a regular panel of people is used.

- **Hall tests**: A random group of people are brought in from the street to test a product and say what they think of it.

- **Observation**: Trained observers watch people to assess their reactions to a street advertisement or in-store goods or display. Observation is also used to check competitors' prices.

⊞ Small businesses and market research

- Small businesses cannot afford to pay for full-scale consumer surveys, but some field research can be carried out quite cheaply. Friends and possible customers can be questioned about a business idea. A short, simple questionnaire could be used.

- Skilful questioning of exhibitors at trade fairs can provide a large amount of data about market trends and new developments.

DESK RESEARCH

- Virtually all the external desk research sources, both official and non-official, are also available to small businesses. Some excellent market reports are published on all types of businesses.

- Trade magazines are full of up-to-date information. Training and Enterprise Councils and Chambers of Commerce can also provide information about local markets and business trends.

QUESTION SPOTTER

Exam questions might be set on the following:
- What is a focus group?
- What part does observation play in market research?
- How could a small toy shop carry out its own market research?

CHECK YOURSELF QUESTIONS

Q1 a What are the two main methods of market research?

b Give one example of each.

Q2 State what kind of research you would use to find the following information:

a the number of people in Britain who own a car

b whether people intend to buy a new car next year

c why some people prefer one newspaper to another

d the circulation figures of daily newspapers

Q3 A manufacturer is planning to introduce a new chocolate bar. Explain the methods of market research the firm might use to see if it would be likely to succeed.

Answers are on page 163.

UNIT 7: MARKETING

▮ Product ▮

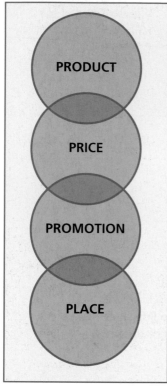

7.1 *The marketing mix*

⊞ The marketing mix

- Market research helps a business to discover what consumers want. **Marketing** helps it to satisfy those wants.

- To market its products profitably, a business has to consider four main factors, known as the **four Ps**.

  1 the **product**, or the kind of good or service provided

  2 the **price**, or what the customer can be charged

  3 **promotion**, or how customers will hear about the product

  4 the **place**, or how the product will be distributed

- The marketing department's task is to mix together the four Ps in the right proportions to obtain the best **marketing mix**.

- It is no good getting only one P right. Each of the four Ps is essential to marketing success. They must be properly mixed so that the whole package appeals to the target consumers in the chosen market segments.

- Packaging is also a very important factor in marketing, to the extent that some experts consider it to be the 'fifth P' (see page 78).

A CONTINUOUS PROCESS

- This mixing process is not a one-off process. It continues throughout the whole life of a product, from the moment it is launched to the moment when it is withdrawn from the market. The marketing mix never ends.

⊞ The product

- Although all the four Ps are important, the **product** is the most important. Without the product, there could be no price, no place, no promotion. The product is the basis of the whole marketing process. Each product has some features which distinguish it from similar products.

⊞ Differentiation of products

- Manufacturers use these features to **differentiate** their goods, or make them different, from their rivals' products. For example:

  - One clothes manufacturer may use better materials than its rivals. Another may have better workmanship.

  - One computer manufacturer may install a 24-hour, unlimited-use hotline for its customers. Another may have its hotline functioning for only eight hours a day.

  - One computer manufacturer may give a one-year guarantee; another may give a two-year guarantee.

⚡ A* EXTRA

Manufactured goods have three main features: objective, such as design and colour; subjective, such as image and status; add-on, such as guarantees and after-sales service.

💡 QUESTION SPOTTER

Exam questions might be set on the following:
▶ Why is the product the most important of the four Ps?
▶ What is differentiation? Give one example of differentiation in a) watches; b) shoes; c) shavers.

- The possibilities of differentiation are almost endless.

- At one time there were many goods, such as milk, which were not differentiated. Now there are skimmed, semi-skimmed, full-fat, extended-life, long-life and other kinds of milk to appeal to various subgroups in the market segment.

⊞ Branded goods

- Branding goods is one of the traditional and most successful methods of differentiation. A **brand** is a trade name which can be used only by the firm that has registered it.

- Brand names are sometimes the name of the firm, such as Heinz or IBM, but more often they are invented names, such as Oxo or Daz.

- Most brands, like McDonald's, are associated with one kind of product, or a range of similar products. A few brand names, however, are associated with a number of very different products. Virgin, for example, is known for its music, its airline and its financial services amongst other things. This is known as **brand stretching**.

BENEFITS OF BRANDING
- Businesses benefit greatly from successful brands. The main advantages are:

  - Constant advertising creates **brand loyalty** among consumers so that sales do not decline.

  - Brand loyalty makes it possible to charge a premium, or higher, price.

  - The brand name makes it easier for the product to be sold globally.

- Brands create **goodwill**, or customer loyalty to the product which has been built up over many years.

OWN-BRAND PRODUCTS
- Branding has been so successful that many of the big supermarkets and high-street stores, such as Tesco and Marks & Spencer, sell their **own-brand products**. These brands are made by other manufacturers. However, they are sold under the retailer's own name. Retailers can sell their own brands at a lower price than the original brands and still make a bigger profit.

7.2 *Product differentiation*

7.3 *Own-brand and branded products*

QUESTION SPOTTER

Exam questions might be set on the following:
- Give one example of a branded good in a) fast food; b) men's clothes.
- State one advantage and one disadvantage of brands.
- Explain why supermarkets have introduced own-brand goods.

? CHECK YOURSELF QUESTIONS

Q1 What are the four Ps?

Q2 A big chain of shops that sells car parts and accessories is considering whether it should sell more own-brand goods instead of selling so many brands. What would be the main advantages?

Answers are on page 164

Product life cycles

▦ The stages of a product life cycle

■ Every product has its own life cycle, the stages through which it passes from the moment it is put on the market until the final moment when it is withdrawn. Life cycles may last for months or for many years.

■ The standard product life cycle is shown in Figure 7.4.

■ There are five main stages in the life cycle:

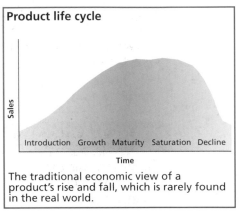

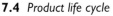

Product life cycle

The traditional economic view of a product's rise and fall, which is rarely found in the real world.

7.4 *Product life cycle*

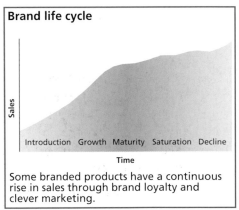

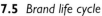

Brand life cycle

Some branded products have a continuous rise in sales through brand loyalty and clever marketing.

7.5 *Brand life cycle*

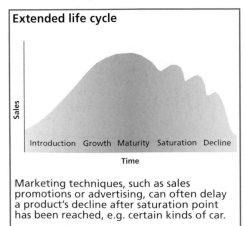

Extended life cycle

Marketing techniques, such as sales promotions or advertising, can often delay a product's decline after saturation point has been reached, e.g. certain kinds of car.

7.6 *Extended life cycle*

- **Introduction**. There is little competition at this stage, because the product is new. However, the costs of developing, making and advertising the product are high, so there is usually a financial loss at this stage.

- **Growth**. Sales start to rise as the product is popular. Costs fall because there are economies of scale in longer production runs. The product starts to make a profit.

- **Maturity**. Sales are still increasing, but at a slower rate. There is greater competition as other firms put rival products on the market.

- **Saturation**. The market is now saturated with many products of a similar kind. Sales start to fall and so do profits.

- **Decline**. Demand starts to shrink and sales fall even further. The point is reached where demand is so low that the product becomes unprofitable and it is withdrawn from the market.

▦ Life cycles of branded goods

■ Many products do not have the standard life cycle shown in Figure 7.4. Some branded goods have a continuous rise in sales over many years (see Figure 7.5). This is obtained by a variety of means, including:

- constantly improving the product quality

- clever marketing techniques, particularly advertising

- brand loyalty

▦ Product life cycle extension techniques

■ Other products do not have the continuous success of some branded goods, but their life can be extended, often for many years, by different marketing techniques (see Figure 7.6). Some of the most important are:

- **Improved models**. Producing a new version of a product is one way of extending its life cycle, for example by bringing out a new version of a camera, or adding a new flavour to a range of crisps (see Figure 7.7). It is cheaper, and less risky, to upgrade a product than it is to produce a new one.

- **More frequent use**. If consumers use a product more frequently, the life cycle will be extended. Shampoo manufacturers would benefit if people could be persuaded to wash their hair more frequently.

- **New uses**. If businesses can find new uses for a product, its decline can be delayed. For example, manufacturers benefited greatly when trainers became fashionable street wear in the 1980s.

- **Packaging**. Changes to packaging are used extensively to extend product life cycles.

The importance of a product range

- One way of making sure that a business as a whole is not badly affected by declining sales is to have a wide **product range**. A product range consists of goods of a similar kind, such as the various models of cars made by a car manufacturer. When the life cycle of one model is coming to an end, the life cycle of another model may still be growing.

- Or a car manufacturer might gain greater protection against declining life cycles by having a wide **product mix** – making goods of different kinds, such as cars, vans, trucks and motorbikes.

7.7 *A vast selection of different-flavoured crisps*

A* EXTRA

It can be dangerous to have too wide a product mix, as the business may become so unfocused that it loses its competitive edge.

? CHECK YOURSELF QUESTIONS

Q1 What are the five stages in the product life cycle?

Q2 Describe the difference between a product range and product mix.

Q3 A firm that makes sets of rubberized table mats finds that sales have declined greatly because people have far fewer formal, sit-down meals at home and eat out more in cafés and restaurants. Suggest how it might extend the life cycle of its product.

Answers are on page 164.

Price

Cost-plus prices

■ Prices are one of the most powerful weapons in modern marketing. In the past, most prices were based on the **cost-plus pricing** method. This was calculated by the following formula:

> unit cost + overheads + mark-up = selling price

■ For example, the total unit cost of a product, including the cost of manufacture (or variable costs) and the overheads (or fixed costs), might be £3. The manufacturer might want a mark-up (or profit) of 25 per cent. The mark-up would be £3 × 25 ÷ 100 = 75p. Therefore, the total price would be £3.75.

Other factors in pricing

■ Old-fashioned businesses still calculate their selling price in this way, but for modern businesses the cost-plus price is just one of the many factors they take into account when they are deciding their prices. Some other basic factors are:

- **Supply and demand.** This has a big influence on prices in the primary sector of production. For example, if potatoes are in short supply, prices will rise; if there is little demand for potatoes, the price will fall.

- **State of the economy.** If the economy is booming, with little unemployment and rising wages and salaries, prices will rise. If there is a recession, with much unemployment, little overtime and businesses closing, prices will fall.

- **Price plateau.** For each kind of good there is a price plateau, or range of price, that careful shoppers think they would have to pay. The price range for a particular product might be from £1.50 to £1.75. If the product is priced below £1.50, many people will think it must be inferior. If it is over £1.75, many people will think it is too expensive.

Modern pricing methods

■ Businesses have to consider all these basic factors in setting prices, but they also use a number of pricing 'tricks'. Some of the main ones are:

- **Complementary price.** One product may be sold at a relatively low price, but the product that goes with it may have a relatively high price. For example, a ballpoint pen might be cheap and the refill expensive.

- **Critical price point.** Goods are rarely priced at £10 exactly, but at £9.99 instead. There is only one penny difference in price, but customers think £9.99 is cheaper because the critical price point of £10 has not been reached.

- **Differential price.** Some stores charge higher prices in small towns than they do in cities, where there is more competition. Some

supermarkets are now considering charging lower prices at times of the day when there are fewer customers.

- **Loss leaders**. These goods, sold at cost price, are often displayed in windows or in wire baskets at the entrance to supermarkets to attract customers into the store.

- **Penetration price**. Retailers may use a penetration price – a very low price – when they open a new shop.

- **Promotional price**. Businesses often use specially low prices for goods that are being promoted in relation to some event, achievement or success.

- **Price cut**. Prices are often cut dramatically to sell slow-moving stock or at the end of a product's life.

- **Sale**. Mark-downs – or sales – were once used mainly at the end of the seasons of the year, but they now take place at all times.

- **Skimming price**. This is a high price which can be charged when a product is first introduced because it has novelty value.

- **Discount price**. A reduction in price, or a discount, may be given for large orders, for cash payments or to loyal customers.

- **Two for the price of one**, or three for the price of two, is another form of discount pricing.

? CHECK YOURSELF QUESTIONS

Q1 Where would you expect to find a loss leader?

Q2 Put an appropriate word or phrase connected with pricing in the following sentences

  a £20 is a _____ .

  b Loyal customers often receive _____ on all their purchases.

  c A _____ may be used when a product is launched.

  d Supermarkets may soon use _____ in slack periods and the rush hours.

Q3 Explain cost-plus pricing and give an example.

Answers are on page 165.

Promotion

⊞ Methods of promotion

- The business world is now so competitive that the third P – **promotion** – has become increasingly important. Promotion is the way in which a business draws attention to itself and its products. There are three main methods:

  1 Advertising

  2 Public relations

  3 Merchandising

⊞ Advertising

- The main reasons for advertising are:

  - factual announcements, such as the opening of a new shop, or telling customers that a product is faulty and asking them to return it

  - persuading people to buy goods or services, e.g. by showing some well-known person using a firm's shampoo in a television advertisement

  - creating a good image of a business or improving it, e.g. by showing how much it cares for the environment

  - altering people's views of a business or an industry, e.g. after it has suffered some disaster such as an outbreak of BSE in cattle

DIFFERENT KINDS OF ADVERTISEMENTS

- Advertisements are of many different kinds. In all, about £12 billion is spent on advertisements in Britain every year. Newspapers and magazines account for over half the total amount spent and television for nearly one-third.

- Advertising has become such a specialized and highly skilled job that large companies usually employ an **advertising agency** to run their campaigns for them.

ADVERTISING MEDIA

- There is a great variety of **media**, or channels of communications, which can be used for advertising. The main channels – and their advantages and disadvantages – are:

CHOOSING THE RIGHT BRANCH OF THE MEDIA

THE PRESS
- Easy targeting of market segments
- Ads can be kept
- Colour available

But
- Not as dramatic as TV or film
- Ads often unread

7.9 *The Grand Prix winner in the IPA Business-to Business Advertising Awards 1998 (Wallis Tomlinson)*

7.10 *Advantages and disadvantages of branches of the media*

> **⚡ A* EXTRA**
>
> The Advertising Standards Authority (ASA) monitors all advertisements (except those on television and radio) to see that they are legal, decent and true.

TELEVISION

- Emotional impact
- Huge audience
- Life-like

But

- Ads can't be kept
- Expensive
- Targeting more difficult than with press
- Viewers often turn ads off

POSTERS

- Immediate impact
- Seen by many people
- 24-hour impact, if illuminated
- National campaigns possible

But

- Limited information
- Difficult targeting
- Only suitable for mass markets

RADIO

- Relatively easy targeting
- Low cost

But

- Small audience

CINEMA

- Very great impact
- Very life-like
- Good targeting

But

- Audience often miss ads
- Limited audience

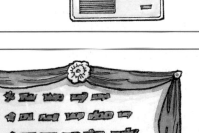

DIRECT MARKETING

- Pin-point targeting possible
- Easy to measure effectiveness of campaign

But

- Opposition to 'junk' mail
- Mailshots often inaccurately targeted

QUESTION SPOTTER

Exam questions might be set on the following:

▸ What are two advantages of newspaper advertisements?

▸ What sort of goods and services would be advertised on television?

▸ What would be the best kinds of goods or services to advertise on the radio?

HANDBILLS

• Can be kept
• Blanket coverage (with door-to-door)

But

• Many thrown away
• Only local

INTERNET

• Global coverage
• Low costs

But

• May be security problems
• Great competition

■ It is most important for businesses to choose the right branch of the media (or mixture of branches) for its advertisements. The choice depends upon a number of factors, including the following:

  • how much the business can afford to spend

  • the kind of message that the advertiser wants to communicate

  • the market segment a business wants to contact

  • whether the likely customers are local, regional, national or international

  • the special qualities that the branch of the media has to offer, such as dramatic moving pictures with a variety of sounds

■ As Figure 7.10 shows, each branch has its own advantages and disadvantages.

▦ Public relations

■ **Public relations** (PR) has two main objectives:

  1 to gain favourable publicity about the organization in various branches of the media free of charge

  2 to present a favourable image of the business and its products

IMAGE CREATION

■ The PR department is responsible for the company image, or what other people and organizations think of it. It uses a variety of methods to improve the company's image, including:

  • sponsorship of sporting, artistic or charitable events

  • help with local community projects

  • talks and demonstrations in schools and colleges

⚡ A* EXTRA

Public relations plays a vital part in big business, as it helps to create and maintain a company's public image by obtaining publicity in the media. Unlike advertisements, no charge is made for publicity. However, the company has to spend thousands of pounds on a publicity department or pay a specialist firm.

COMPANY LOGOS

- A **logo** is a picture or a symbol that represents the company. Logos are important because they

  - make it easy for people to recognize the organization

  - establish a brand identity

  - create an appropriate image

- A company can spend hundreds of thousands of pounds on getting the right brand name and logo. Specialist design agencies usually do the work. British companies spend about £150 million a year on rebranding themselves.

⊞ Merchandising

- **Merchandising** is a means of attracting consumers to a product and persuading them to buy it.

POINT-OF-SALE PROMOTIONS

- One of the most common forms of merchandising is **point-of-sale (POS) material**. Examples include:

  - posters

  - showcards

  - display stands and cases

  - dump bins – wire or plastic containers filled with goods often used for loss leaders near store entrances

  - wire racks, like those at checkouts filled with chocolate bars

  - moving or illuminated displays in-store

  - pavement models, such as a butcher or a fishmonger outside a shop

METHODS OF PROMOTING SALES

- **Sales promotions** are another form of merchandising. Some of the most common methods are:

  - **Free gifts**: air miles, gift tokens with petrol.

  - **Special offers**: three pence off a bar of chocolate, £100 trade-in on a new cooker, two for the price of one or three for the price of two.

  - **Discount vouchers**: a few pence off the next jar you buy.

  - **Bonus packs**: bigger amounts for the same price.

  - **Charity promotions**: donations to charity for each product bought.

  - **Competitions**: free scratch cards and bingo cards.

  - **Loyalty cards**: a number of points for every pound you spend.

- Usually, sales promotions produce only a short-term increase in sales. Consumers buy the product while the offer lasts, and then switch to a product with a new offer or back to their favourite brand.

7.11 Company logos

CHECK YOURSELF QUESTIONS

Q1 What are the main advantages of newspaper advertisements?

Q2 David and Sue are opening their first restaurant in a London suburb.

   a How could they advertise their restaurant?

   b What would be the main advantages?

   c What else could they do to attract customers?

Q3 **a** Describe one kind of sales promotion.

   b Give two examples.

   c What is the main disadvantage of sales promotions?

Answers are on page 165.

■ Place and packaging ■

▦ Place and channels of distribution

- The last of the four Ps – **place** – deals with how a business distributes its products. There are four main **channels of distribution**, which link the producer, or seller, with the consumer, or buyer.

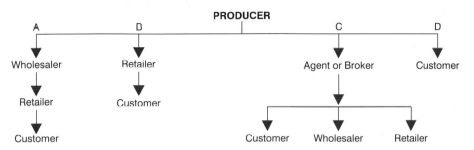

7.12 *Channels of distribution*

WHOLESALERS

- The traditional way of distributing goods is shown as Channel A in Figure 7.12. The wholesaler buys goods in bulk, or large quantities, from manufacturers. They are then split up into smaller quantities and delivered to the retailer. This process is known as **breaking bulk**.

- Sometimes, retailers collect their own goods by buying them at cash-and-carry warehouses.

- The main benefits of wholesalers are that all three businesses – the producer, the wholesaler and the retailer – can concentrate upon their specialized work. Manufacturers' transport costs are reduced, as they have to deliver goods only to wholesalers instead of to hundreds of shops. Retailers can order small quantities, which enables them to stock a much greater variety of goods.

DISTRIBUTION DIRECT TO RETAILERS

- This channel of distribution is shown as Channel B in Figure 7.12. It is used by supermarkets and by other multiple stores that have set up their own distribution systems for transporting goods to their branches (see page 80). It is also used by the manufacturers of some branded consumer goods and durable consumer goods, such as furniture.

- The main advantages are that it cuts out the wholesalers' profit and gives producers greater control over the marketing and distribution of their products.

AGENTS AND BROKERS

- These are shown as Channel C in Figure 7.12. Agents and brokers usually deal direct with customers, or sometimes with wholesalers or retailers.

- **Agents** usually do not own the goods or services they deal in. They take a **commission**, or a percentage of the selling price, on every sale.

- Agents are found in many kinds of business. Most houses and package holidays are sold direct to the customer through estate agents and travel agents respectively.

▷ What is a wholesaler?
▷ Explain the term 'breaking bulk' and give one example.
▷ Describe the benefits wholesalers provide for retailers.

QUESTION SPOTTER

Exam questions might be set on the following:
- ▷ What is a wholesaler?
- ▷ Explain the term 'breaking bulk' and give one example.
- ▷ Describe the benefits wholesalers provide for retailers.

QUESTION SPOTTER

Exam questions might be set on the following:
▶ Why do supermarkets have their own distribution systems?
▶ What is a commission? Give two examples of people who receive them.
▶ Why are agents useful for exporters?

■ Agents are also used by firms who want to sell their goods abroad without going to the expense of setting up a complete sales organization in a foreign country. An agent, who is a native of the country, can help the exporter greatly through his or her knowledge of the country's markets, customs and laws.

■ **Brokers** deal in a variety of goods in the primary sector of production, such as tea, zinc and sugar. Like agents, they usually do not own the goods they deal in, but take a commission on what they sell. There are other brokers: stockbrokers, who deal in company shares, and insurance brokers, who sell insurance policies to private and business customers.

DIRECT MARKETING

■ With **direct marketing**, goods are sold direct to the consumer. This is shown as Channel D in Figure 7.12. This method of distribution is increasingly used in many different kinds of business because there is often a great saving in costs. Some of the most common methods are:

- **Factory shops**: manufacturers set up shops on factory outlet sites to sell end-of-line stock and other goods at reduced prices.

- **Direct mail**: contacting potential customers direct by sending advertising material through the post.

- **Telephone calling**: either in response to a request or 'cold calling' people at random. Favoured by double-glazing firms.

- **Internet**: the World Wide Web is one of the fastest-growing methods of direct marketing.

- **Teleshopping**: goods are shown on cable TV and ordered on the phone.

- **Mail–order catalogues**: this is one of the oldest methods. Credit payment facilities make this method popular.

- **Press advertisements**: these advertise goods or services and include a post-paid reply coupon.

- **Magazine inserts**: booklets or leaflets enclosed in magazines advertising goods and services.

A* EXTRA

▶ Direct mailing is often so poorly targeted that it is known collectively as 'junk mail'. However, it is so cheap, and response rates can be measured so accurately, that it continues to be widely used.
▶ Direct marketing gives producers greater control over the marketing and the distribution of their goods and avoids wholesalers' and retailers' charges.

⊞ Packaging: the fifth P

■ Packaging plays such a powerful part in the marketing mix that it has become known as the 'fifth P'. There are three main aspects of packaging:

1 the materials from which it is made, such as paper, cardboard, plastic, glass, etc.

2 the size, shape and weight of the container

3 the label

PRODUCT

- With many goods, the package is an essential part of the product. For example, liquids could not be sold without leak-proof containers of some kind, e.g. bottles for disinfectants.

- Packaging can be used to extend product life cycles. Changes can be made to:

  - the container, such as changing the size or shape of a bottle

  - the packaging material, e.g. using plastic instead of paper

  - the design on the packaging, for example using gold instead of red paper and including a free-offer coupon

7.13 *Packaging used to extend product life cycles*

PRICE

- Elaborate packaging helps to persuade customers to buy products. It is often a significant part of the total price.

PLACE

- Packaging plays an essential part in the distribution of goods. It should be strong and secure, and easy to handle and transport. It should also be of a suitable shape and size for easy and attractive display in shops and stores.

PROMOTION

- Packaging is used to promote the brand name, which is usually prominently displayed. It can also be used to advertise details of other promotions, such as price cuts, competitions, special offers, etc.

OTHER USES OF PACKAGING

- The bar code on the package plays an essential part in the automatic re-ordering of stock in supermarkets and other big stores.

- Packaging also provides information required by law, such as the ingredients of tinned food.

CRITICISMS OF PACKAGING

- Consumers frequently complain that packaging is difficult to open. This is partly caused by the need to stop people tampering with the contents. Environmental pressure groups complain that fancy packaging wastes scarce raw materials. Much packaging is now recycled and used again. By law, local councils will have to recycle 25 per cent of household waste by 2005, and the European Union now obliges industry and retailers to recover at least 52 per cent of packaging.

QUESTION SPOTTER

Exam questions might be set on the following:
- How can packaging be used to prolong a product's life cycle?
- What are the environmental objections to packaging?
- What actions have the government and the European Union taken to reduce the environmental effects of packaging?

? CHECK YOURSELF QUESTIONS

Q1 What benefits do wholesalers provide for manufacturers?

Q2 Describe what kinds of direct marketing a hotel could profitably use.

Answers are on page 166.

REVISION SESSION 1

Retailing

QUESTION SPOTTER

Exam questions might be set on the following:
▸ What is a multiple retailer?
▸ How do you account for the success of supermarkets?
▸ Why have many supermarkets moved out of high-street locations?

⊞ The dominance of supermarkets

■ In all, there are nearly 300,000 retail outlets in Britain, over half of which are owned by people with just one shop. There are fewer than 150 multiple retailers with more than 100 stores and shops each. Yet the multiples' combined turnover now accounts for well over half of total retail sales.

■ Today, supermarkets dominate the grocery trade. The big four – Tesco, Sainsbury, Safeway and Asda – are all in the Top 100 list of British companies. In all, they employ about half a million people.

■ Supermarkets' biggest stores are on new **out-of-town** shopping and leisure sites, so that most people now do their big weekly shop by car.

■ On these out-of-town sites, supermarkets have greatly extended their range of goods and services.

⊞ New methods of distribution

■ At one time, manufacturers and wholesalers delivered goods in a variety of vans and lorries to high-street retailers, who stored the goods on their premises until they could be sold.

■ Distribution accounts for up to a quarter of the shelf-price of fast-moving consumer goods, like milk, breakfast cereals and coffee. Therefore, supermarkets needed the most efficient distribution system if they were to save costs and keep their shelf-prices low.

■ Supermarkets pioneered new methods of distribution. This involved setting up their own big **regional distribution centres (RDCs)** at central points throughout the country. Manufacturers delivered their goods to the RDCs, which were then distributed to all the supermarket's shops and stores in that region. This method of distribution is shown as Channel B in Figure 7.12 on page 77.

■ This method of distribution not only saves costs by cutting out the wholesaler's profit, it also gives supermarkets greater control over suppliers and distribution.

■ Some of the RDCs are run by specialist distribution firms, which also supply the vehicles and drivers. Vans and lorries of many different sizes, including refrigerated lorries for frozen food, are provided. The vehicles are painted in the retailer's distinctive livery, or colour, with the name and logo on the sides.

■ This system of distribution has been so successful that it has been adopted by other kinds of multiple retailers with large numbers of branches.

8.1 *Supermarkets on out-of-town sites have extended their range of goods and services*

ADVANTAGES OF NEW DISTRIBUTION METHODS

■ The RDC system of distribution has many advantages.

- New electronic systems in supermarkets have made it possible to keep a second-by-second check on the remaining stock of goods in each store. Replacement stock is ordered automatically from the RDCs and delivered **just-in-time**, or just before the old stock runs out.

- Electronic ordering of goods saves both time and money.

- Just-in-time deliveries reduce costs. Like all businesses, supermarkets borrow money to finance the purchase of stock. They have to pay interest on these loans. The shorter the time they hold stock, the less interest they have to pay.

- Smaller stock needs less storage space, which reduces rents.

- Bulk deliveries from the RDCs also cut costs, as handling charges, or the cost of loading and unloading goods from vehicles, is reduced.

- Reduced handling of goods means that there is less damage in transit and less chance of theft.

- Bulk deliveries also bring economics of scale. Bigger lorries are much more cost-effective than smaller lorries.

⊞ Supermarkets versus small shopkeepers

■ Supermarkets have become such a powerful force in retailing that it has become increasingly difficult for small shopkeepers to compete.

ADVANTAGES OF SUPERMARKETS

■ Supermarkets – and other multiple retailers – have many advantages.

- They benefit from many economies of scale – buying, financial, marketing, administrative and distribution.

- They have much higher turnovers, so they can afford to have lower profit margins.

- They can afford to have lower mark-ups on own-brand goods.

- They have diversified and offer a much wider range of goods and a growing number of services.

- There is plenty of space on out-of-town sites for free customer car parking.

- They have long opening hours, with some staying open 24 hours a day.

ADVANTAGES OF SMALL SHOPKEEPERS

■ Although many small shops have closed, sole proprietors do have some advantages compared with bigger retailers. The main ones are:

- There is a growing number of voluntary buying groups – like Spar and Londis – that buy goods in bulk for all their shopkeeper-members, so that they can sell at lower prices to their customers.

QUESTION SPOTTER

Exam questions might be set on the following:
▸ What is an RDC?
▸ What is just-in-time delivery? State one advantage.

QUESTION SPOTTER

Exam questions might be set on the following:
▸ How do supermarkets benefit from economies of scale?
▸ What use do supermarkets make of diversification?
▸ Why is it difficult for small shopkeepers to compete successfully against supermarkets?
▸ Why are niche markets advantageous for small shopkeepers?

▶ Many small shops and post offices have closed, particularly in the country, but some have been saved by collective village ownership and by a new breed of young entrepreneurs who have given up city life to run a country business.

▶ Small businesses are also more flexible than larger firms, have greater personal knowledge of their customers, and can spend more time catering for their needs.

- They often have cheaper rents and much fewer administrative overheads.

- They can provide a better quality of personal service.

- They can give credit to their regular customers.

- They can try to find profitable niche markets.

OTHER ADVANTAGES OF BEING SMALL

- If small businesses improve their marketing techniques, they can become even more competitive. Therefore, they can adapt and change their businesses much more quickly.

- Small businesses can tailor their products much more closely to their customers' needs. Grocers can stock the special items that the supermarkets do not sell. In suitable areas, they can compete on quality, too, by stocking local produce or more upmarket goods.

- They can offer better customer service by delivering goods to their customers' homes and they can also offer better advice to their customers.

? CHECK YOURSELF QUESTIONS

Q1 State two goods and two services which out-of-town supermarkets provide.

Q2 What are the main advantages for retailers of cutting out the wholesaler?

Answers are on page 166.

Banks and finance houses

The functions of financial institutions

■ The main financial institutions are:

- high-street banks and merchant banks

- finance houses

- building societies

- insurance companies and pension funds

■ These institutions provide vital financial services for both consumers and businesses of all kinds. Their main functions are to:

- act as an essential link between savers and borrowers

- provide most of the external finance for all kinds of businesses

- buy most of the shares that are issued by public limited companies

- provide exchange services for foreign currencies and financial links with the rest of the world

- handle the financial transactions of consumers and businesses

High-street banks and finance houses

■ The logos of the Big Four banks are familiar sights everywhere.

■ There are also a smaller number of other English, Irish and Scottish banks operating in England, plus a number of newcomers such as building societies that have become banks, like the Halifax, and supermarket banks, like Sainsbury's.

■ Every day, the **high-street banks** handle up to nine million cheques. They 'clear' them by checking if there is sufficient money in the account of the **drawer**, who has written the cheque, before the amount is transferred to the account of the **payee**, to whom the money is being paid. That is why these banks are also known as **clearing banks**.

■ In addition, the banks handle millions of other transactions, such as customers paying money into their deposit accounts or paying interest on their loans. This money which the banks obtain over the counter is known as **retail funds**.

■ Banks also obtain **wholesale funds** on the **money markets** from companies and other financial institutions that have cash to spare.

QUESTION SPOTTER

Exam questions might be set on the following:
▸ State two financial institutions that provide services for large companies.

8.2 *The Big Four high-street banks*

A* EXTRA

It is much more expensive to use retail finance as the bank has to provide expensive high-street branches, pay staff and keep elaborate records of all transactions.

SERVICES FOR BUSINESS

■ High-street banks provide a full range of services for businesses, including:

- current and deposit accounts of various kinds

- overdrafts, loans of many kinds and mortgages

- insurance, both business and personal

- foreign exchange dealing

- advice on starting, running and expanding businesses

SMALL BUSINESS CRITICISMS OF BANKS

■ Small businesses more often criticize high-street banks than praise them. They complain that:

- bank profits are far too high

- charges on small business accounts are excessive

- banks are more interested in short-term profit than long-term support

- they are unwilling to take many risks in financing new ideas

- there are too many mistakes in accounts, which are often in the bank's favour

- delays of up to a week in clearing cheques cost small businesses much money

MERCHANT BANKS

■ The Big Four banks all have merchant banking departments. There are also separate **merchant banks**.

■ Some of their main functions are:

- arranging share issues for public companies that want to raise additional capital

- negotiating finance for companies that want to take over another company

- managing investments for company pension funds

FINANCE HOUSES

■ **Finance houses** provide funds for both businesses and private people for the hire purchase of vehicles and equipment. Their interest charges are usually higher than those for bank loans.

⊞ Building societies

- **Building societies** provide mortgages for people of all socio-economic groups and a great mix of other services, including savings accounts of all kinds, insurance and foreign currency.

- Most building societies are **mutual societies**, which are owned by their members and do not exist to make a profit. In recent years, they have faced increasing competition from banks that have also gone into the mortgage business.

- Recently, some of the biggest societies, with the agreement of their members, have converted into banks and become public limited companies.

CHECK YOURSELF QUESTIONS

Q1 What is the difference between a bank and a building society?

Q2 Explain why it is cheaper to raise wholesale funds than retail funds.

Q3 Describe two factors that may have made high-street banks unpopular with many small businesses.

Answers are on page 167.

UNIT 9: PRODUCTION

Products and methods

⊞ Creating new products

■ New products are the life-blood of any business, which keep it healthy and alive.

■ New products are usually made because:

- a new need or want has been identified by market research

- the firm's research and development department has invented some new product, process or material

- very often, an existing product is redesigned

■ To succeed, new products must be suitable for their purpose and have certain other qualities. The most important ones are:

- reliability

- safety

- good design and attractive appearance

- ease of use

- ease of maintenance

■ Products that possess all these features will be of high quality and likely to succeed.

⊞ The work of the production department

PRODUCTION MANAGER'S FUNCTIONS

■ In addition to seeing that the quality of the product is maintained, a **production manager** also has the following duties:

- to design a suitable plant layout with sufficient storage space for the method of production being used

- to see that production flows freely and that machines and workers are fully employed

- to make sure that production schedules are maintained so that goods are produced on time

- to make out a production budget and to ensure that costs are kept within the budget

---

⚡ A* EXTRA

If a product is unreliable, it will damage the firm's reputation and increase costs through the need to provide constant replacements of defective parts.

PURCHASING MANAGER'S FUNCTIONS

■ In very small manufacturing firms, the production manager will be in charge of buying all the raw materials and any components which are bought in from other manufacturers. In larger firms, there will be a **purchasing manager**, whose main tasks are:

- to buy all the raw materials, components and other goods or services
- to make sure that they are high in quality and low in price
- to see that suppliers keep up the standard of the parts and components they supply, and to provide training for their workforce if necessary
- to establish a suitable computerized system for ordering stock and controlling its storage and movement
- to make sure that the goods and services are delivered when required

QUESTION SPOTTER

Exam questions might be set on the following:
▶ State two duties of a production manager.
▶ Why do large firms have a purchasing manager in addition to a production manager?

⊞ Methods of production

■ There are three main ways in which goods can be produced:

1 **Job production**: one product is made at a time, and then another product is made.

2 **Batch production**: a quantity of one product is made, followed by a quantity of the same, or another, product.

3 **Flow** or **mass production**: the product is made continuously on an assembly line.

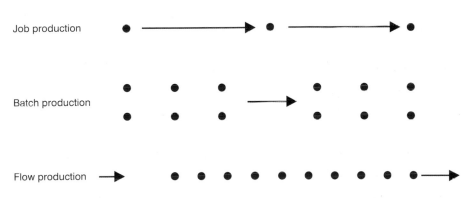

9.1 *Job, batch and flow production*

■ These methods, which are a favourite exam topic, will now be considered in more detail. Make sure that you do not confuse these production processes with the chain of production, described in Unit 1.

⚡ **A* EXTRA**

Job satisfaction is always high with this method of production because workers can use their individual skills to produce goods of which they can be proud. The engines of Aston Martin cars are signed individually by the craftsman who built them by hand.

9.2 *Batch production of bread in British Bakeries' bread plant at Erith Bakery, which manufactures over 10,000 loaves per hour*

9.3 *Speciality loaves require more labour-intensive production methods than standard bread*

💡 **QUESTION SPOTTER**

Exam questions might be set on the following:
▸ State one advantage and one disadvantage of job production.
▸ What is batch production? Give one example of where it might be used.

JOB PRODUCTION

- **Job production** involves making a single item, usually to a customer's specification or detailed description of the product required. These are sometimes one-off orders, which may or may not be repeated at a later date.

- Job production is always expensive because it involves the work of highly skilled craftspeople; the quality of materials and workmanship is high; and there are few economies of scale. The work may be done by one person alone, as with a suit. Or a large number of skilled workers may be involved, as with building a cruise liner or an aircraft.

- In a factory, the production process is always centred on the product. With large products, such as an aircraft, groups of skilled craftspeople work together on and in the product as it is being made.

- The main advantages and disadvantages of job production are:

Advantages	Disadvantages
• extremely flexible	• high cost of goods and labour
• high-quality products	• few economies of scale
• job satisfaction	• may be delays between orders

BATCH PRODUCTION

- **Batch production** occurs when a quantity of one product is made, followed by another batch of the same product or by a batch of a different product. The production process is not continuous.

- For example, in a bakery, the batches of loaves go through several different stages of production. Some speciality loaves may need more labour-intensive treatment than standard loaves.

- There is less specialization in this type of production. In job production, each skilled worker is usually responsible for doing one particular job.

- In batch production, however, some workers may be only semi-skilled, and most of them do only part of the whole job. For example, in a clothes factory, some workers may cut out the material; others may machine, or stitch, the garment; and another group may finish the garments.

- With heavier or bigger products, the work is usually done in stages by separate sections. The semi-finished products have to be moved from one section to another; and the machines have to be reset to do each new job.

- The production manager must ensure that similar machines are grouped together in the right production order so that as little time as possible is wasted. This is called **layout by process**.

- The main advantages and disadvantages of batch production are:

Advantages	Disadvantages
• more flexible	• difficult to manage efficiently
• lower wages, as workers are less skilled	• workers may be less motivated
• cheaper, as there are some economies of scale	• storage costs of unfinished goods

FLOW PRODUCTION

- **Flow production**, which is sometimes called **mass production**, is used to produce large quantities of the same consumer goods at high speed.

- Heavy products are moved on a conveyor belt or assembly line from one group of semi-skilled workers to another, so that workers have to keep up with the movement of the line.

- There is intense division of labour, with each worker doing just one small job. Most of the work is semi-skilled, and machines are used as much as possible instead of manual labour.

- **Layout by product** is used, with machines and assembly workers placed along the line in the right order for the assembly of the product.

- The main advantages and disadvantages of flow production are:

Advantages	Disadvantages
• great economies of scale produce low unit costs	• high capital costs
• low labour costs	• one fault in assembly line can halt all production
• little training required	• lack of worker motivation
• continuous production all day and night if needed	

A* EXTRA

Flow production is capital intensive, because very expensive plant and machinery is used with a small workforce.

QUESTION SPOTTER

Exam questions might be set on the following:
▸ What is another name for flow production?
▸ State one advantage and one disadvantage of flow production.
▸ Explain which kind of goods you would expect to be made by this production method.

CHECK YOURSELF QUESTIONS

Q1 State two of the main methods of production and give one example of each.

Q2 Explain how firms benefit by changing over to a mass production system.

Q3 Adrian was working on an assembly line when his firm closed down. He went on a course to train as an electrician, and then obtained a job in a factory making helicopters. What differences would he find in his new job?

Answers are on page 168.

New mass-production methods

⊞ Disadvantages

- In addition to those listed on page 89, there were further defects with the traditional form of mass production.

  - It was expensive to produce different versions of the basic product, as this entailed stopping the assembly line and resetting machines.

  - It was necessary to hold a large buffer stock of raw materials, components and parts, as the lack of one item could bring the whole assembly line to a halt.

  - The boredom of workers often resulted in poor-quality work and industrial disputes.

- In the last 20 years or so, most of these defects have been remedied by improved methods of production.

⊞ Improved methods

- The main changes have been:

  - more automation

  - more efficient stock control

  - new team-working methods

AUTOMATION

- Automation involves increasing the number and variety of machines used so that very little manual labour is used in the production process. Furthermore, it is easy to keep the factory open for 24 hours a day.

- Computers are at the heart of these new production processes. They enable the design, manufacture and management of production to be linked together into one whole process (see Unit 13). Computers make it much easier to adjust and reset machines while they are operating.

JUST-IN-TIME STOCK CONTROL SYSTEMS

- Computers have also transformed stock control systems. Some manufacturers buy in many of their parts and components. It is therefore important to have a highly efficient method of stock control and delivery.

- Modern factories now use **just-in-time** stock control systems. Computers keep a constant check on the level of all stocks and order them automatically from suppliers just before they are required. The suppliers deliver the parts to the factory's storage areas. They are often transported from there to the assembly line in computer-controlled, driverless trucks.

⚡ **A* EXTRA**

Some of the most highly automated plants are found in the oil, plastics and chemical industries. Many have flexible manufacturing systems so that, for example, quite small quantities of different-coloured paint can be produced without stopping the production line.

- The workforce sometimes has no more than two hours' amount of stock by the line. This means that any delay in supplies may stop production. Manufacturers, therefore, need suppliers who are totally reliable and capable of delivering goods just-in-time.

TEAM-WORKING METHODS

- Automation and just-in-time deliveries have helped to increase productivity and lower costs. They have also created new team-working methods.

- Production is centrally controlled by computers, but it is split up into separate processes, each of which is done by a team of workers – or **cell** – with its own team leader. Large objects are assembled on moving assembly lines, but smaller goods, such as fluorescent light fittings, are assembled at benches.

⊞ Quality control

- **Quality control** has become of increasing importance in all businesses because it is one of the main ways of satisfying customers.

- Products are checked for such factors as:
  - fitness for purpose
  - lack of defects
  - safety
  - design and appearance

9.4 *'Cell' manufacturing of wheel components*

TOTAL QUALITY MANAGEMENT

- To achieve even higher standards of quality, some mass production companies have introduced a new system of **total quality management (TQM)**. Under this system, both samples of the products and the machines used in making them are checked at regular intervals throughout the shift. This ensures a much higher-quality product.

THE FUNCTIONS OF QUALITY CIRCLES

- **Quality circles** play an essential role in TQM companies. They are small, voluntary groups of employees who meet regularly to discuss ways of improving their work.

- Quality circles usually have between five and 12 members. They investigate any problems associated with their work and suggest solutions. If management approves the proposals, they are put into practice.

9.5 *Quality control of musical instruments*

- The circle members also need to be trained in problem-solving and team work.

- In a big company, there may be 100 separate quality circles in all departments, from accounts to production.

Exam questions might be set on the following:
▸ Why is quality control important in a manufacturing business?
▸ What is the main purpose of total quality management?
▸ Describe what quality circles do.

RESEARCH AND DEVELOPMENT

- Another way of improving the quality of existing products, and developing new ones, is through **research and development**, or **R&D**, as it is more commonly known.

- R&D involves scientific research into ideas for new products, new versions of present products, production processes and raw materials.

- If it is decided to go ahead with the project, it is then developed into a practical product that can be marketed. Development often takes longer, and costs more, than the research.

? CHECK YOURSELF QUESTIONS

Q1 What is just-in-time? State one advantage.

Q2 State two disadvantages of traditional methods of flow production.

Q3 Explain the likely effects of introducing total quality management in a manufacturing firm.

Answers are on page 168.

UNIT 10: PEOPLE IN BUSINESS

Job motivation

⊞ Why do people work?

- What makes people work? What motivates them? Throughout the whole of the 20th century and into the 21st, writers on management and other topics have tried to answer these questions, but they have been unable to reach any general conclusion.

FREDERICK W. TAYLOR

- Frederick W. Taylor (1865–1915), an American writer, believed that workers were naturally lazy and were motivated only by money. Their work needed to be planned for them; they should be told what to do.

ELTON MAYO

- Elton Mayo (1880–1949) was the founder of the human relations school of management. He believed that money was not the sole motivation. Workers wanted some part in making decisions and wanted to gain satisfaction from their work. His emphasis was on the worker rather than work, and people and their relationships rather than jobs.

DOUGLAS MCGREGOR

- Douglas McGregor, an American writer, published a book in 1960 describing the two main attitudes towards workers, which he called Theory X and Theory Y.

- Theory X assumed that workers
  - are lazy
  - lack ambition and responsibility
  - must be forced to work
  - want money and security

- Managers who believe in Theory X refuse to delegate, or give up, some of their own power to other people. They like to tell other people what to do; to reward and punish; and to keep a firm control over employees.

- Theory Y assumes that workers
  - like work
  - want responsibility
  - can exercise self-control
  - are not motivated only by security

- Managers who believe in Theory Y like all employees to have a say. They want to encourage people to work on their own or in a team, and are willing to delegate.

> ⚡ **A* EXTRA**
>
> Taylor's book, *The Principles of Scientific Management*, published in 1911, had a great influence on managers for many years – and still does in some firms. In it, he conceived of a method for shortening the amount of time a task took by studying workers doing the task and removing 'non-productive time'.

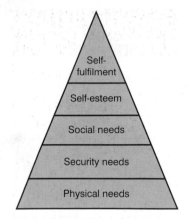

10.1 *Maslow's hierarchy of needs*

⚡ *A * EXTRA*

Companies recognise this need for self-esteem by giving people important-sounding titles, such as 'Director of Corporate Development', and material symbols of success, such as bigger cars and larger offices, and for top executives, chauffeur-driven cars.

▦ The hierarchy of needs

■ Abraham Maslow (1908–1970), an American psychologist, developed a general theory of motivation which he called the hierarchy of needs. He designed a model, shaped like a pyramid, with the most essential needs at the base, rising to a peak as each need was satisfied.

■ Maslow's hierarchy identified five needs:

1 Physical needs: the most basic – the essential need of food, warmth and shelter.

2 Security needs: connected with the home, the family and a sense of safety.

3 Social needs: concerned with personal relationships, being part of a group, a sense of belonging.

4 Self-esteem: important for people to feel happy with what they have achieved.

5 Self-fulfilment: when all these other needs are satisfied, there is the final need for self-fulfilment, a sense of personal achievement and growth.

▦ Job improvement schemes

■ Many companies have introduced **job improvement** schemes for manual workers. There are three main kinds:

1 **Job rotation.** In this system, workers do one simple job for a time and are then transferred to another simple job to provide variety in their work.

2 **Job enlargement.** This is a horizontal extension of work, which increases the number of tasks that workers do as part of their normal routine.

3 **Job enrichment.** This involves a vertical extension of work. For example, a railway worker might be in total charge of a small station: issuing tickets, loading freight on to trains, seeing that it is safe for the train to leave, etc.

⊞ Increased unemployment

- For the last 25 years or so, **unemployment** has been a major problem in Britain, particularly in the recession of the early 1980s.

- There are a number of different causes of unemployment. The main ones are:

  - **cyclical unemployment** caused by **recessions**, or slumps in economic activity, which are followed by booms, or increases in economic activity, which provide more jobs again

  - **structural unemployment** in declining industries, such as coal mining, shipbuilding and steel making

  - **technological unemployment** owing to increased automation, which replaces workers by machines

  - **frictional unemployment** caused while employees are finding new jobs. This is often due to **increased global competition**, which forces businesses to cut costs

CUTTING COSTS

- One of the simplest ways for a company to cut costs is to get rid of as many employees as possible. This reduces labour costs and increases **productivity**.

- To cut costs even further, many companies have also established a **flexible workforce** in which full-time jobs are replaced by temporary, part-time or short-term work.

  - **Temporary work.** In some big companies now, up to ten per cent of the workforce are 'temps', who are employed only if there is a particular job to be done.

  - **Part-time work.** There has been a huge rise in part-time jobs of all kinds, which have increased four times to nearly 5.5 million in the last ten years. About 42 per cent of working women have part-time jobs compared with 7.5 per cent of men.

  - **Short-term contracts.** Employees are given a short-term contract for a year or eighteen months, instead of a permanent job. This means that employers can dismiss them at the end of the contract without having to pay any compensation.

🔆 QUESTION SPOTTER

Exam questions might be set on the following:
- ▸ What are the five main levels in Abraham Maslow's hierarchy of needs?
- ▸ Explain how companies might use one of the needs to motivate its workforce.
- ▸ Describe the kind of managers who support Douglas McGregor's Theory X.
- ▸ How could a supermarket use job improvement schemes to make work more interesting for its employees?

⚡ A* EXTRA

At one time, part-time workers had few rights. New government regulations in 2000 gave part-time workers the same rights as full-time workers in pay, pensions and annual holidays — proportionate to their shorter hours of work.

? CHECK YOURSELF QUESTIONS

Q1 What effect might job improvement schemes have on workers' attitudes to their job?

Q2 Describe two forms of unemployment.

Q3 Explain the differences that a flexible workforce can make to a company.

Answers are on page 169.

Pay and benefits

⚡ A* EXTRA

The government has introduced a national minimum wage for workers which is currently £4.10 an hour for workers over 22, and £3.50 an hour for workers between 18 and 22.

▦ How rates of pay are decided

■ There are great differences in the rates of pay in Britain. At the bottom of the scale, nearly five per cent of all full-time employees earn less than £160 a week, while some employees, such as City dealers, earn £20,000 a week, and a few people, such as top models and professional footballers, earn £40,000 a week, plus profitable sponsorship deals.

EFFECTS OF SUPPLY AND DEMAND

■ Rates of pay are still decided to a large extent by the forces of supply and demand. Generally, pay will be low if the work can be done by almost anyone.

OTHER FACTORS AFFECTING PAY

■ Other factors that can affect pay include:

- length of training

- level of qualifications

- the power of the employee's trade union or professional body

- working conditions, including health or safety risks

- whether it is a manual or a non-manual job

▦ Manual workers' pay

💡 QUESTION SPOTTER

Exam questions might be set on the following:
▸ What is another name for a manual worker?
▸ Explain the meaning of 'time rate'.

■ **Manual workers** – or blue-collar workers – are people who work mainly with their hands. They are paid wages, usually weekly, which are based on a fixed rate of pay, or **time rate**, for a set number of hours a week. For instance, a manual worker might be paid £8.20 an hour for a 36-hour week, or £295.20 a week.

COLLECTIVE BARGAINING

■ In some industries, trade associations, representing employers, and trade unions, representing employees, use **collective bargaining** to decide national rates of pay for all the manual workers in their industry. Every year, representatives of each side negotiate and come to an agreement on
- the hourly rate of pay

- additional payments, such as overtime

- the length of the working week

- other working conditions, such as the length of holidays

■ Collective bargaining has big advantages for employees. A trade union has much greater bargaining power than individual workers. It represents thousands of workers; it can speak with one voice; and it has trained, highly skilled negotiators.

- It also has some advantages for employers, which is why collective bargaining is still used by some major British companies. The advantages are that it:
  - makes it simpler to administer wages
  - gives pay stability for a year at least
- Its main disadvantages are that it:
  - pays all workers the same basic wage, whether they work hard or not
  - gives great power to the unions
  - weakens managers' opportunity to make decisions

QUESTION SPOTTER

Exam questions might be set on the following:
- Who is involved in collective bargaining?
- What is decided by bargaining at plant level?
- Describe one advantage of collective bargaining for a) employers; b) employees?

LOCAL BARGAINING

- Working conditions on the shopfloor vary so much that additional payments have always been made at regional or plant level. These are negotiated by union representatives and management.

- There can be a lot of hard bargaining over pay at local level. Very often, the unions are forced to accept a **productivity deal**, in which higher wages are paid only in return for greater productivity.

EXTRA PAYMENTS FOR MANUAL WORKERS

- In addition to their basic pay, most manual workers receive a number of other payments. Two of the most important are:

  1 **Overtime pay**. This is one of the most common forms of extra payment. For additional hours, workers usually receive pay of time and a half. Overtime has advantages for employers as it allows them to produce more goods when order books are full without the expense of recruiting extra workers.

  2 **Shift premium payments**. About 15 per cent of manual workers also receive extra pay for working anti-social shifts late at night or early in the mornings when most other people are not working.

PAYMENT BY RESULTS

- With time rates, workers get the same pay however hard they work. This payment system may cause problems as it encourages workers to work less hard during normal hours so that they get time and a half for working overtime.

- Many companies, therefore, also use a **payment by results** system, which links additional pay with what workers produce. About one-third of all full-time manual workers receive some form of payment by result. There are many different versions.

  - **Piecework**. In piecework, workers are paid for each item they produce. Time rates and piecework rates are often combined. The normal time rate is paid up to a certain level of output and piecework after that. With all piecework pay systems, there is a danger that workers may cut corners to produce more goods, so an efficient inspection system is essential.

QUESTION SPOTTER

Exam questions might be set on the following:
- What is one advantage of overtime for a) employees; b) employers?
- What extra payments do some workers receive for working anti-social hours?
- Are there any other ways in which manual workers might be motivated apart from extra pay?

- **Bonuses**. Workers may be paid a bonus when they exceed a certain production target. For example, they might be paid extra if they produced more than 2,000 ladders in a day. The bonus needs to be high enough to motivate the workers.

- **Profit-sharing**. In some factories workers are paid an annual bonus, which is based on the company's profit. Bonuses of this kind do not provide a strong personal motivation to work hard, as they are not specifically linked with individual effort.

▦ Non-manual workers' pay

- **White-collar employees**, who do not usually work with their hands, are paid salaries. These are based on an annual rate of pay, divided into twelve equal parts. Salaries are paid monthly by cheque or bank transfer.

- Some salaries in the public sector are decided by collective bargaining. There is usually an **incremental pay scale**, with regular annual increases.

- There are big disadvantages with an incremental pay system. Employers have to give an employee a rise every year, even if he or she does not really deserve it. Employees get no further pay rises once they have reached the top of their salary scale.

PERFORMANCE-RELATED PAY

- In the private sector, most salaried employees now have a personal **contract of employment**, with no automatic pay rises. Increases in pay are given only for better performance. A manager assesses an employee's performance at an annual **appraisal**. This is often based on targets and objectives that have been agreed by the manager and the employee.

ADDITIONAL PAYMENTS FOR SALARIED EMPLOYEES

- Most salaried employees get some additional payments. The most important are:

  - **Increases for inflation**. Rises are usually given every year to help cover inflation.

  - **Cost-of-living allowance**. In London and other big cities, where living is more expensive, a cost-of-living allowance may be given to salaried staff.

  - **Bonuses**. Many salaried employees receive annual bonuses based on their own, their department's or their firm's performance.

  - **Commission**. Some employees receive commissions, or percentage payments, on everything they sell. Commission is usually paid with the salary. For example, some sales assistants in stores receive one per cent commission on all the goods they sell.

  - **Overtime**. Most salaried employees, such as teachers, work much longer hours than the number stated in their contract of employment, but receive no overtime payments. A small percentage of salaried employees, such as police constables, get overtime pay.

⊞ Gross and net pay

- Under **PAYE**, or the **pay-as-you-earn** system, employers have to make certain deductions from all employees' **gross pay**, whether they receive salaries or wages. Gross pay consists of the basic pay plus any additional payments, such as overtime.

- Employers deduct the amounts due for income tax and National Insurance contributions. There may also be voluntary deductions, such as contributions to a company pension. The amount that is left, after all these amounts have been deducted, is the **net pay**, or take-home pay.

- The personnel department is responsible for working out the gross and net pay for each employee every week or month and giving each employee a **pay slip**, showing the gross pay and the deductions.

QUESTION SPOTTER

Exam questions might be set on the following:

▸ What is a white-collar worker?
▸ Explain the differences between wages and salaries.
▸ Describe the differences between gross and net pay.
▸ What additional payments could be made to salaried staff to increase their motivation?

GROSS PAY		DEDUCTIONS				
SCALE PAY	1,537.50	INCOME TAX	270.68	TAX CODE 178L		TAX BASIS 0
		NAT. INS	109.77	TAX WK/MTH 02	TAX REFUND HELD	
		PENSION	44.91			
				FOR TAXING ONLY		
				CUMULATIVES TO DATE		
				EARNINGS		3,075.00
				TAXABLE PAY		2,985.18
				TAX		541,12
				NIC		219.54
				PENSION		89.82
TOTAL GROSS PAY	1,537.50	TOTAL DEDUCTIONS	425.36	NET PAY 1112.14		

'-' after an amount indicates a DEDUCTION. 'R' after an amount indicates a REFUND

10.2 *An employee's payslip*

⊞ Fringe benefits

- Most employees, both waged and salaried, also receive a number of **fringe benefits**. These are goods or services that are provided free by the employer. Employers benefit because fringe benefits increase motivation. Employees also gain because they pay either no tax at all on the fringe benefit, or only a proportion of the tax they would have paid on an equivalent increase in pay.

FRINGE BENEFITS FOR MANUAL WORKERS

- Some of the main fringe benefits for manual workers are:

  - **Pension schemes.** These help to keep employees working for the company.

  - **Discounts on purchases** of the firm's goods or services. These are cheap for employers to provide.

  - **Free bus services to work.** This ensures that employees get to work on time.

  - **Subsidized canteen meals.** These are popular with employees.

  - **Free uniforms,** which give employees a sense of affiliation or belonging to the company.

QUESTION SPOTTER

Exam questions might be set on the following:
▸ Give one example of a fringe benefit for a) manual workers; b) salaried employees.
▸ What is the main advantage of a fringe benefit for a) manual workers; b) salaried employees?
▸ Describe the fringe benefits an executive of a large company might receive.

- Big companies provide many more fringe benefits for salaried staff. The higher the employee's rank, the more fringe benefits he or she may receive. Companies often use a package of pay and fringe benefits to poach top managers from other firms.

- Practically all companies provide staff with pension and sick-pay schemes, and sometimes with private health insurance, often for all members of the family.

- The company car is still one of the most popular fringe benefits, even though the tax charged for its use has risen steadily in recent years.

- Luncheon vouchers, which can be used to pay part of the cost of a meal, are another popular 'perk'.

- Other fringe benefits for executives include: the use of company flats in London and other capitals; large expense accounts; foreign trips, sometimes accompanied by their partner; cheap loans and mortgages; payment of school fees; relocation, or moving, expenses.

- There are even more valuable benefits. Many top managers have an option to buy shares in their company at a fixed price, which gives them huge profits if the price of the shares rises. Others receive many thousands of pounds when they join, or leave, a company – **golden hellos** and **golden handshakes**.

Employee welfare schemes

- Some welfare services are provided mainly for female employees. Special provisions have to be made as many women often do two or three other unpaid jobs as well as their paid job – looking after the children, the house and aged or sick relatives. Workplace crèches, or nurseries, are now provided by some big companies.

FLEXIBLE WORKING PATTERNS

- Women also benefit greatly from flexible working patterns, such as only working in term time, which have been introduced by a number of progressive employers.

- Some of the main flexible working patterns are:

  - **Flexitime**: with flexitime, employees work for an agreed number of hours every day – core time – but can then work the rest of their hours when they choose.

  - **Term-time working**: employees work only during the school terms and have unpaid leave during the school holidays.

- **Annual hours**: some employees now work a set number of hours in a year, e.g. 1,976 hours a year instead of 38 hours a week. This gives both the employer and the employee greater flexibility.

- **Job sharing**: two people share the same job. One might work in the morning, the other in the afternoon; or they might work alternate weeks.

- **Career breaks:** these breaks are usually unpaid and can last for up to five years. They may be taken to look after young children or to study for a higher qualification.

CHECK YOURSELF QUESTIONS

Q1 What would be the likely effects if a company ended collective bargaining in all its factories?

Q2 Describe the differences between bonuses and commissions.

Q3 How is net pay calculated?

Answers are on page 169.

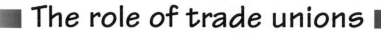

The role of trade unions

⊞ Functions of trade unions

- The main functions of **trade unions** are to:

  - negotiate rates of pay and conditions of work with employers

  - give members legal advice and assistance about such matters as health and safety at work, unfair dismissal and equal opportunities for men and women

  - give financial help to members in strikes or after accidents at work

  - provide a range of other services, such as mortgages, insurance, personal loans and discounted holidays

DECREASE IN TRADE-UNION MEMBERSHIP

- By law, everyone has the right to belong to a trade union. Membership, however, has fallen dramatically in recent years. It is now only 7.2 million, less than a third of all employees.

- There are now almost as many union members among salaried staff, such as bank employees, as there are among manual workers. There are also nearly as many women as men in trade unions. Membership of trade unions is high in the public sector.

⊞ Industrial action

- A trade union's main power is **industrial action**. The main types of action its members can take are:

  - **Non-co-operation**: members refuse to use a new machine or to accept new working methods.

  - **Work to rule**: members may work to rule by observing all the official working rules, which they normally ignore, such as checking a machine every time it is used. This will slow down production greatly.

  - **Overtime ban**: most manufacturing firms rely heavily on overtime to fulfil their production schedules. An overtime ban would hurt the firm, as it would not be able to fulfil its orders, but it would also hurt the workers, as they would lose their higher rate of overtime pay.

  - **Strike**: a withdrawal of labour is the union's final weapon. This can range from a token strike of a few hours to a selective strike by key workers, to an all-out strike by the whole workforce.

- Industrial action has a powerful effect on a firm as it reduces or stops its production of goods or services, which affects its cash flow and its profits. It also damages the firm's reputation.

⚡ A* EXTRA

Trade-union rights to take industrial action were greatly reduced by Conservative governments between 1979 and 1997. Unofficial strikes were banned, workers had to vote for official strikes in secret ballots, only six pickets were allowed at factory gates and secondary picketing by outside sympathisers was banned. These restrictions still apply.

⊞ Single union agreements

- One of the biggest workplace problems for many employers is having to negotiate with more than one union. This often means that one union will use the pay rise awarded to another union as the basis for an even higher pay award for its own members.

- In the past, there were also frequent **demarcation disputes** between rival unions over which union should do which job.

- To avoid problems of this kind, some companies have negotiated **single union agreements**, in which one union represents all the workers in negotiations over pay and working conditions.

- The main benefits for employers are:
  - easier negotiations, as there is only one union to deal with
  - reductions in negotiating time and administrative costs
  - fewer conflicts between unions

NEW-STYLE AGREEMENTS

- These single union agreements are sometimes part of a whole new-style deal. These were introduced into Britain by Japanese companies. In addition to single union agreements, they usually include:

  - **Single-status employment**: the traditional differences between managers and workers, between 'them' and 'us', is ended. Manual workers have the same hours of work, holidays, canteens and car-parking facilities as white-collar workers.

  - **Labour flexibility**: all workers do any job that they are capable of doing.

  - **Team work**: there is a greater emphasis on team work and co-operation between all grades of employees.

  - **No-strike agreements**: the union agrees not to strike. Both management and union agree to accept the decision of an arbitrator, or independent judge, in any dispute.

⊞ Employee protection

- An enormous number of laws have been passed to protect the health, safety and rights of employees. Some of the most important are:

  - **Equal Pay Act 1970**. Employees doing equal work, or, from 1984, work of equal value, must receive the same pay as employees of the other sex.

  - **Sex Discrimination Act 1975**. There must be no sexual discrimination in employment, training or recruitment.

QUESTION SPOTTER

Exam questions might be set on the following:
- Give two examples of industrial action.
- What is a demarcation dispute?
- Explain how employers benefit from single-union agreements.

⚡ A* EXTRA

Manual workers' status and motivation are increased in new-style agreements as they are treated more fairly. Management also benefits, because administration is simplified and there is a greater sense of corporate unity.

QUESTION SPOTTER

Exam questions might be set on the following:
- State two acts which protect employees.
- What are the main provisions of the Health and Safety at Work Act?

- **Race Relations Act 1976**. People must not be discriminated against in employment, training and recruitment because of their colour, race, nationality or ethnic origins.

- **Employment Protection Act 1978**. Employees must be given a written contract of employment. They must not be dismissed unfairly, i.e. without a reasonable cause. They must receive redundancy pay if they have been working for the firm for two years or more and their job is abolished.

HEALTH AND SAFETY AT WORK

- The Health and Safety at Work Act 1974 is one of the most important laws. Under this Act, employers must provide safe premises and machinery, and make sure that employees' health is not affected by their work. Employees also have an obligation to take care of their own and their fellow workers' health, and can appoint their own safety representatives. The Health and Safety Executive employs inspectors to see that the law is carried out.

? CHECK YOURSELF QUESTIONS

Q1 State one effect of a demarcation dispute on a firm.

Q2 What are the differences between a work to rule and an overtime ban?

Q3 If any employer refuses to recognize unions, what effects would it have on employees?

Answers are on page 170.

UNIT 11: RECRUITMENT AND TRAINING

Recruitment

▦ The work of the personnel department

■ Most companies with more than 100 employees have a **personnel department**, which deals with all the relations between the employer (or the management) and the employees. In some bigger companies, it is now called the human resources department.

■ The personnel department deals with a wide range of matters, including recruitment.

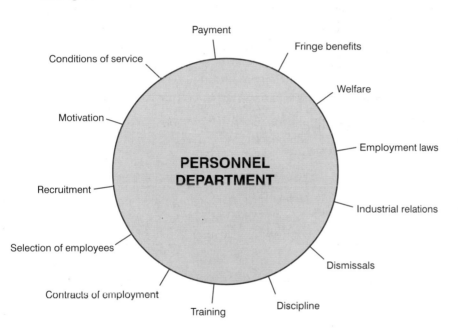

11.1 *The work of the personnel department*

▦ Reasons for recruitment

■ Employees may be needed when:

- the business expands

- the business targets a new market

- new skills are needed because of technological advances

- employees are dismissed or retire or leave to join other firms

■ The decision to appoint a member of staff is usually made by the personnel department and the head of the department or section concerned. Decisions to appoint heads of departments and very senior managers would be made by the directors of the business.

⊞ First stages in recruitment

- The personnel department's first task is to carry out a **job analysis** by deciding the exact nature of the job, and the knowledge, skills and other qualities required to do it.

JOB DESCRIPTION

- The personnel department would then produce a **job description**. This describes the nature of the job and the responsibilities involved, usually in great detail. The job description is useful for informing applicants exactly what the job entails, and also for settling any later disputes about the tasks that the person appointed has been asked to perform.

JOB SPECIFICATION

- A **job specification** is also written, stating the qualifications, skills, previous experience and other personal qualities that the person must have.

⊞ Methods of external recruitment

- Most job vacancies are filled by recruiting people from outside the firm. There are several methods of external recruitment for a job. They include:

  - **Personal recommendation**. Someone who is already working for the firm recommends someone they know. This takes place at all levels of business.

  - **Jobcentres**. These are a nationwide chain of government agencies, which have details of local job vacancies and of a smaller number of jobs elsewhere. They deal mainly with manual and office work. They also provide other services for the unemployed, such as details of training courses.

  - **Private employment agencies**. They provide firms with details of selected employees, including temporary staff, for a fee. There are general agencies, which deal with all kinds of staff, and specialized agencies for some kinds of work, such as catering and nursing.

  - **Executive employment agencies** provide a complete recruitment service for senior managers, for a large fee.

  - **Careers advisers** in schools and colleges, and university appointment boards, may be able to provide suitable candidates.

  - **Advertisements**. This is one of the most common methods of obtaining employees.

ADVERTISING JOB VACANCIES

- A job advertisement should:

  - describe the job fully, and the skills and qualifications required

  - indicate what is being offered in the way of training, fringe benefits, career prospects

  - be legal, i.e. it must not discriminate between male and female applicants, or against people of ethnic origins

11.2 *A private employment agency*

CHOICE OF MEDIA

■ Job advertisements range from a sole proprietor's card in a shop window, costing a few pence a week, to a company's display advertisement in a quality national newspaper, costing hundreds of pounds for just one insertion.

■ It is important to choose the most appropriate newspaper or magazine for the kind of job. It is easy to find out from the publication about their readers. This helps the personnel department to choose the most suitable publication.

- Quality national newspapers are used mainly for advertising senior managerial and professional vacancies in both the private and the public sectors.

- Business and professional magazines are used mainly for specific technical and professional posts.

- Local newspapers are used for a variety of local jobs at all levels, ranging from the unskilled to senior management (see Figure 11.3).

The selection process

SENDING OUT APPLICATION FORMS

■ An **application form** has to be designed which can be sent to people who apply for the post. Most personnel departments have a standard form that is suitable for all vacancies.

■ The application form, and further details about the post and the firm, are sent to everyone who replies to the job advertisement. The application form usually asks for the following information:

- personal details, including age and nationality

- education and training, including schools, colleges or universities attended and qualifications obtained

- previous employment, including wages or salaries and reasons for leaving

- health, including any serious illnesses and whether registered as a disabled person

- reasons for applying for the post

- interests and leisure activities

■ It also asks for the names of previous employers and responsible persons who could give a **reference**, or a written statement about the applicant's ability and character. Applicants are sometimes asked to write a letter of application and to enclose a **curriculum vitae (CV)** – an outline of their career – instead.

EXPERIENCED CENTRE LATHE TURNER REQUIRED
For further details please contact:
Jed Barker
Precision Tools
Duncombe Industrial Estate
Cannock
Staffs
Tel 01889 555666

OFFICE ADMINISTRATOR
Full/part-time position
Good keyboard and telephone skills essential.
£4.50 per hour
Contact Sue: 01543 494957

PRACTICE NURSE REQUIRED
FOR BUSY 10-DOCTOR PRACTICE
Basic hours Monday to Friday
8.30-4.30, day off Wednesday,
alternate Saturdays 9am-12 noon,
29 hours per week, Grade E1.
Practice Nurse experience preferred.
Please apply in writing enclosing full C.V. to:
The Practice Manager
The Health Centre
Whitecross
Rugeley
Staffs WS12 8PQ

11.3 *A selection of job advertisements*

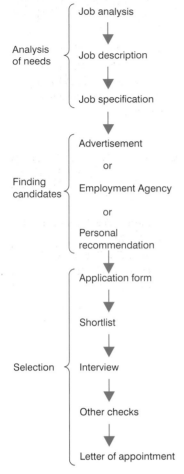

Analysis of needs
- Job analysis
  ↓
- Job description
  ↓
- Job specification
  ↓

Finding candidates
- Advertisement
  or
- Employment Agency
  or
- Personal recommendation
  ↓

Selection
- Application form
  ↓
- Shortlist
  ↓
- Interview
  ↓
- Other checks
  ↓
- Letter of appointment

11.4 *The recruitment process*

QUESTION SPOTTER

Exam questions might be set on the following:
- What is a CV?
- Describe the recruitment process from job analysis to final choice of candidate.
- Why do some firms use other methods of selection in addition to interviews?

MAKING A SHORTLIST OF CANDIDATES

- When all the completed application forms have been received, members of the personnel department study them to find the most suitable candidates.

- A number of candidates will be put on a **shortlist** and invited to attend an **interview**.

INTERVIEWING THE CANDIDATES

- An interview is usually the main feature of the job selection process. Sometimes there is just one interviewer, but, more often, there are two or three. With senior jobs, there is normally a panel of interviewers.

- Interviews give the interviewers the chance to meet the candidates, to assess their abilities and characters, and to see how they react to one particular situation – the interview itself. Interviews do not always indicate whether a person will be successful in the job, as they do not test the skills and qualities that would be required for that particular post.

- There are other defects in the interview system. Some candidates are much more successful in the interview than they would be in the job. Interviewers sometimes let their personal prejudices influence their choice of candidate.

OTHER METHODS OF SELECTION

- Many firms, therefore, use other methods of selection in addition to the interview. With some jobs, they test the candidates' skills.

- With other jobs, they use **personality tests**, which are based on questions written by a psychologist.

- With management jobs, there might be whole-day tests of endurance and qualities of leadership in outdoor activity centres.

- Companies also carry out other checks. Most companies send for the references that the candidate has provided, and other companies confirm with the examining board whether degrees and certificates have actually been awarded. A medical examination is also carried out for some jobs.

⊞ Advantages and disadvantages of external recruitment

■ There are advantages and disadvantages with external methods of recruitment. The main ones are:

Advantages	Disadvantages
• large choice of candidates	• long process of recruitment, selection and appointment
• new individuals with new ideas	• costly advertising and/or agency fees
• applicants may have wide experience	• difficulties in assessing suitability of candidates
• greater flexibility in amount of salary offered	

⊞ Internal recruitment

■ In **internal recruitment**, a job is offered only to current employees by advertising it on staff notice boards or in the company news sheet or magazine.

Advantages	Disadvantages
• much cheaper	• limits number of candidates
• much quicker	• no 'new blood' or ideas
• abilities – and failings – of individual already known	• may cause jealousy
• employee has good knowledge of the firm and its policies	• managers may resent loss of staff to other departments
• provides a career structure	• employees may resent receiving orders from former equal
	• may create another vacancy to be filled

⚡ A * EXTRA

Internal recruitment may make the company unproductive if all the top posts are filled by long-serving employees with few new ideas.

☀ QUESTION SPOTTER

Exam questions might be set on the following:
▶ State one benefit and one drawback of internal recruitment.

? CHECK YOURSELF QUESTIONS

Q1 How does a job description differ from a job specification?

Q2 How would you recruit a senior manager?

Q3 State two advantages of internal recruitment compared with external recruitment.

Answers are on page 171.

⊞ Contract of employment

■ When a person has been appointed, the employer must give him or her a written statement of employment – or **contract of employment** – within two months. Some of the items that must legally be included are:

- the name and address of the employer

- the employee's name

- job title or brief description of job

- the date employment began

- the amount of pay and the intervals between payments

- hours of work

- holiday entitlement

- sick leave arrangements

- pension arrangements

- length of notice for ending employment

- if not a permanent job, the period for which employment is expected to last

- details of disciplinary and grievance procedures (see Figure 11.5)

QUESTION SPOTTER

Exam questions might be set on the following:

▸ When must an employee be given a contract of employment?

▸ State two items which must be included in a contract of employment.

▸ Describe the topics which might be covered in an induction programme in a large company.

DISCIPLINARY PROCEDURE

Procedure – Formal stages

Prior to enacting each of the following stages the employee will be given the opportunity of being accompanied by a colleague or, where appropriate, a chapel official.

Appeal process

The employee may appeal by written request to the Human Resources Department. An appeal must be lodged within 5 working days of the warning having been given.

STAGE 1 – ORAL WARNING

Any employee whose conduct or attendance does not meet acceptable standards will be given an oral warning by his or her Manager. He/She will be told the reason/s for the warning and what improvement is required. The warning will remain on the employee's file for a period of 12 months.

STAGE 2 – WRITTEN WARNING

If the required improvement identified in Stage 1 is not forthcoming or in the event of other unsatisfactory conduct or attendance a disciplinary interview will be arranged by the Manager. If the explanation by the employee is unsatisfactory, a written warning will be issued by the Human Resources Department. This will state:- the nature of the complaint, the improvement being looked for, the time for the improvement achieved, the likely outcome if improvement is not achieved. The warning will remain on the employee's file for a period of 12 months.

STAGE 3 – FINAL WRITTEN WARNING

If the terms of a Stage 2 Written Warning fail to produce the required improvement or in the event of other unsatisfactory conduct or attendance a further disciplinary interview will be arranged. The employee will again be invited to offer an explanation which will be fully considered prior to a decision being taken on an appropriate course of action. An unacceptable explanation will result in a Final Written Warning being given which will specify the same type of detail as stated in a Stage 2 warning. N.B. If misconduct or attendance is sufficiently serious to warrant only one warning, Stage 3 will act as the first and final warning. The warning will remain on the employee's file for a period of 12 months.

STAGE 4 – DISMISSAL

Failure to meet the required terms of Stage 3 warning or in the event of other unsatisfactory conduct or attendance will result in a final interview with the employee who once more will be given the opportunity to explain the reasons why he/she has not responded to previous warnings. Unless the explanation after fullest consideration is accepted, dismissal will result. A decision to dismiss must be finally authorized by the most Senior Executive in the employee's Division (after consultation with Human Resources).

SUMMARY DISMISSAL FOR GROSS MISCONDUCT

The following list which is by no means exhaustive nor in any order of severity provides examples of offences which are regarded as Gross Misconduct: theft, fraud, deliberate, falsification of records, fighting, assault, deliberate damage to Company property, being under the influence of alcohol or drugs during working hours or on company premises, serious negligence which causes unacceptable loss, damage or injury, wilful intimidation. Employees suspected of Gross Misconduct will not be allowed to continue working and will be suspended on salary whilst the alleged offence is investigated. If, on completion of the investigation and the appropriate disciplinary procedure, the Company is satisfied that Gross Misconduct has occurred, the result will be summary dismissal without notice or payment in lieu of notice.

11.5 *Disciplinary and grievance procedures*

⊞ Induction programmes

- With all externally recruited people, one important task is to give them some form of induction. This introduces them to their job, their new colleagues, the premises and the firm.

- In a big company, there is usually an elaborate, formal induction programme. This usually involves a talk on the company's history, products and policies. The company's organization will be explained, and the new employee will be shown the building where he or she will work. The recruit will be told the company's rules and given a copy of the staff handbook. There may also be a tour of various departments. Finally, new employees will be introduced to managers and colleagues.

- An induction programme helps to make recruits familiar with the company and the working environment.

- The employer benefits, too, as recruits learn how the company operates. The induction programme presents the company in a favourable light, which may help to increase employee loyalty and motivation.

⊞ Discipline and dismissals

DISCIPLINARY PROCEDURES

- Under the Employment Protection Act of 1978, it is illegal to dismiss an employee without a reasonable cause. Therefore, the contract of employment includes details of the company's **disciplinary procedures** (see Figure 11.5).

- If a company wants to dismiss an employee for unsatisfactory work or misconduct, he or she is usually given a verbal warning first. This is followed by a second warning at a formal meeting with a manager; and finally, a third warning in writing, before the employee is dismissed.

- The contract of employment also says what employees should do if they have a grievance. It gives the name of the person they should see first, and the procedure they should follow if they are still not satisfied.

DISMISSALS

- In most cases, employees can be dismissed only after the whole disciplinary procedure has been observed. Employees must be given the period of notice specified in their contract of employment.

- Employees may be dismissed without notice only if they are guilty of a gross breach of contract, such as theft. They are then entitled only to the pay they have earned up to the time of their **dismissal**.

REDUNDANCY

- Employees can be made **redundant** if their job is being abolished. Employers cannot use this as an excuse for dismissing workers. Firms sometimes use **natural wastage** instead of **compulsory redundancy**, i.e. not replacing employees when they leave or retire.

- The business has to pay compensation, or **redundancy pay**, to employees with at least two years' service.

Exam questions might be set on
the following:
▸ Describe a typical
  disciplinary code.
▸ What is redundancy pay and
  when must it be given?
▸ When might an employee go
  to an employment tribunal?

⊞ The work of employment tribunals

■ The personnel department has to make sure that all the laws relating to employees are observed. Those dealing with equal rights and dismissal are particularly important. If employees believe they have been treated unfairly, they can take their case to an **employment tribunal**.

■ These informal tribunals have a legally qualified chairperson, plus one trade union member and another member from an employers' organization. The most common cases concern unfair dismissal. At present, the tribunal can award a maximum compensation of £50,000, except in cases involving sexual or racial discrimination.

? CHECK YOURSELF QUESTIONS

Q1 In what circumstances could an employee be dismissed without notice?

Q2 What might be the effects on employees if there were no induction process?

Answers are on page 171.

▧ Training ▧

⊞ Why do people need training?

- **Training** is the responsibility of the personnel department. There are many reasons for training employees. The main ones are:

  - general skills shortage, particularly of people with knowledge of computers and information technology

  - inadequate knowledge and skills of individual employees

  - the complexity of the job

  - retraining needs, e.g. mothers returning to work and long-term unemployed

  - introduction of new working methods or machines

  - reducing the need for supervision

  - cutting workplace accidents

⊞ Benefits and drawbacks for firms

ADVANTAGES

- Apart from the obvious benefits of higher production, improved quality of products and a reduction in customer complaints and returned goods, there are other benefits for firms that provide extensive training programmes.

  - **Less absenteeism.** It becomes easier to retain staff, as they feel that they can progress in their career by remaining with the company. There is less absenteeism – employees taking time off work, often without a genuine reason.

  - **Lower labour turnover.** There may also be a lower labour turnover. This is the number of employees who leave in a year expressed as a percentage of the total workforce.

DISADVANTAGES

- Training has some disadvantages for firms. Some employees who have just been trained may leave for better-paid jobs elsewhere. However, they are less likely to do so if the firm provides a clearly defined career structure.

- Training is extremely expensive and takes a lot of company time. It may also increase staff's expectation of promotion.

⊞ On-the-job training

- **On-the-job training**, or **internal training**, is organized by the personnel department and is usually given by members of the firm, though outside specialists may also be called in.

> ⚡ **A* EXTRA**
>
> A high labour turnover can create a general sense of insecurity among a company's employees and give the firm a bad name which makes it difficult to obtain new employees. Costs will also increase, as recruits have to be trained.

Exam questions might be set on the following:
▸ What is one disadvantage of training by a fellow worker?
▸ Why might employees prefer off-the-job training?

TRAINING NEW EMPLOYEES

■ New employees must be given training in their job. This may be nothing more than informal on-the-job advice from a colleague. Although this method costs the firm nothing, it has great disadvantages as the colleague may be passing on inefficient methods of working to the new employee.

■ More efficient firms provide proper training programmes, which are given by skilled instructors.

▦ Off-the-job training

■ Some **external training**, or **off-the-job training**, is provided by colleges and other educational institutions. They provide courses which are designed to meet the needs of local businesses or which lead to recognized qualifications.

■ External training provided by the public sector usually costs firms far less than courses provided by the private sector, which are usually extremely expensive.

GOVERNMENT TRAINING SCHEMES

■ The government or government-sponsored bodies provide many kinds of training. The government has set up **Training and Enterprise Councils (TECs)** in England and Wales to give advice on training and to encourage enterprise.

CHECK YOURSELF QUESTIONS

Q1 a What is the meaning of labour turnover?

b If a firm employed an average of 5,000 workers and 361 left during the year, what was the rate of labour turnover to the nearest whole number?

Q2 Name:

a one advantage of training for employers;

b one advantage of training for employees.

Answers are on page 171.

UNIT 12: COMMUNICATION

Good communication

⊞ What is communication?

- **Communication** is simply a method of sending a message from one person or group of persons to another.

- Good communication will ensure that all persons and organizations understand the message sent.

- Bad communication will have exactly the opposite effect. People will be confused by the message and less likely to do what the business wants.

- That is why good communication is so essential. It is not only *what* you say (or write), but *how* you say it that is important. Your message should be easy to understand and take account of the receivers' own attitudes and feelings.

ONE-WAY AND TWO-WAY MESSAGES

- Communication may be one way, when no reply is wanted or expected. For example, a public notice stating 'TURN OFF LIGHTS' is a command or an order which does not demand a response.

- Most communications are two way, with some **feedback**, or response, required from the receiver.

- If some official response was wanted, a **memorandum**, or a brief written message on a form, would have to be sent.

- The sender could ask for the message to be acknowledged, or for the heads of departments to report what action they were taking to put the order into effect.

- If the sender wanted to make the message more persuasive, a reason for the request could be given, which might be the need to reduce costs.

DIRECTIONS OF COMMUNICATION

- Within any organization, the character of the communication varies according to whether it is going downwards, upwards or sideways.

- The main uses of **vertical downwards communication** are:
  - to give orders or instructions
  - to provide, or ask for, information

- The main uses of **vertical upwards communication** are:
  - to describe the results of actions
  - to provide information that has been requested
  - to make requests or appeals

- The main uses of **horizontal, or sideways, communication** are:
  - to keep equals informed of actions taken, or results achieved
  - to discuss means of tackling problems together

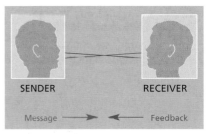

SENDER   **RECEIVER**

Message ⟶ ⟵ Feedback

12.1 *Two-way communication*

Johnson, Patel & Company Ltd

MEMORANDUM

To: All heads of department   **Date:** 18/03/99

From: Kirat Patel   **Reference:** KP/SW

Subject: Lights

It's come to my attention that lights have been left switched on in the offices that are not in use. In one case lights in the conference room were left on overnight.

This wastes energy and money. In the interests of cutting costs, it's vital to ensure that staff in each department turn off all lights when offices are no longer being used.

Please let me know how you plan to proceed.

12.2 *A memorandum is used for internal communication*

13.3 *Visual aids summarize information in a striking way*

⊞ Channels of communication

■ There are three main channels of communication. They are:

1 spoken

2 written

3 electronic

■ **Visual aids**, such as charts, graphs, diagrams, photographs and other illustrations, are often used to support messages. They summarize information and present it in a striking way.

WHY COMMUNICATIONS FAIL

■ There are a number of reasons why communications fail. The cause may be the fault of:

- the sender
- the receiver
- the choice of channel

■ Sometimes the **sender** is to blame. The message may not be clear and accurate or simple enough to be understood by the receiver.

■ The **receiver** may be unwilling to take in the message because they are too busy, or because they have made up their mind already, or because they are too prejudiced to hear the message clearly.

■ The choice of **channel** may also be the cause. For example, it would be no good trying to discuss a very complex contract with a colleague unless he or she had been given a written copy of the contract – preferably well in advance of the meeting. The written channel is more suitable for complicated matters than the spoken channel.

? CHECK YOURSELF QUESTIONS

Q1 Why is feedback important in communication?

Q2 State two reasons why a communication might fail.

Answers are on page 172.

Methods of communication

⊞ What methods are used?

- A variety of methods are used in each of the three channels. Some are used mainly for internal communication, while others are used mainly for external communication. Those which are very commonly used for both internal and external communication are marked with an asterisk (*) in the sections below.

⊞ Internal communication

SPOKEN MESSAGES

- Advantages: Can provide instant feedback; opportunity for discussion.

- Disadvantages: Often costly to arrange in both time and money; frequently no permanent record.

- **Face-to-face meetings***

  - It is estimated that managers in companies spend almost half their time in meetings. They may be one-to-one or group meetings.

  - At large formal meetings, there is a written **agenda**, or a list of items to be discussed. **Minutes**, or a written record of what was said and agreed, are usually kept.

  - There are also many external meetings with customers, suppliers, bank managers, advisers, etc.

  - Meetings are useful because they allow instant feedback and discussion to take place.

- **Presentations***

  - A manager, often accompanied by members of his or her staff, uses a presentation to explain a project or a plan to colleagues. Visual aids are often used to illustrate points in the talk. Presentations are also given externally to clients or potential clients.

  - Presentations allow a large amount of complex information to be communicated to a number of people at the same time. They also provide opportunities for feedback and discussion.

WRITTEN MESSAGES

- Advantages: Permanent record; suitable for both simple and complex messages.

- Disadvantages: Usually takes some time for message to arrive; slow feedback, or sometimes none at all.

- **Public notices** are a cheap way of communicating the same information to a large number of people. However, notices may not be read; and, even if they are, they may be ignored.

- **Memorandums**, or **memos**, are still one of the main means of communication within a business. They are useful for making arrangements or requests and sending confirmations.

> ### ⚡ A* EXTRA
>
> Face-to-face meetings give a general impression of the other person and their attitudes and reactions, but they are often an unreliable guide to a person's true worth and integrity.

12.4 *Personal computers have revolutionized business communications*

- **Reports** are widely used in business. Visual aids, such as charts and photographs, are often used to illustrate them. There is a standard format for a report. It should include a title, a brief introduction, headings or subheadings for each section, a conclusion, a list of recommendations, and the name of the author(s) and the date.

- **Staff bulletins** or **magazines**. Many big firms publish bulletins or larger magazines to give employees information about the company.

ELECTRONIC MESSAGES

- Advantages: Speed; accuracy; quick or instant feedback; message is usually – or can be – recorded.

- Disadvantages: Expensive; whole systems sometimes crash.

- **Telephones** were one of the earliest means of electronic communication and are still widely used for both internal and external communication.

- **Personal computers (PCs)**, which process data at enormous speed, have revolutionized communication and many other aspects of business.

- **Computer software**: By using different kinds of software, PCs can perform a variety of tasks, including **word-processing** letters and documents; storing information on a **database**; and making financial calculations with a **spreadsheet**.

LOCAL AREA NETWORKS

- Firms can link all the computers in the same building to form a **local area network (LAN)**. The computers can communicate with each other and also share common facilities, such as a printer. The PCs are all linked to a more powerful computer, or **server**, which stores a vast amount of information.

- A LAN makes it much easier for managers to access information from other departments and also to keep a check on the work that their staff are doing.

External communication

SPOKEN MESSAGES

- Advantages: Can provide instant feedback; opportunity for discussion.

- Disadvantages: Often costly to arrange in both time and money; frequently no permanent record.

- **Face-to-face meetings** (see page 117).

- **Presentations** (see page 117).

- **Interviews** are usually used for external purposes, such as interviewing a possible employee or a supplier, but they are sometimes used internally on formal occasions, e.g. in internal promotion.

- **Talks**. Formal talks are sometimes used to publicize the firm's activities at trade or public meetings. They are also given internally on induction courses.

- **Annual general meetings (AGMs).** Companies have to hold a general meeting for their shareholders every year. Shareholders are told about the company's financial results and activities during the past year and its plans for the future. They are invited to elect or re-elect directors and to vote on other matters. Any shareholder has the right to question the board of directors. In practice, very few private investors ever attend AGMs.

WRITTEN MESSAGES

- **Advantages:** Permanent record; suitable for both simple and complex messages.

- **Disadvantages:** Usually takes some time for message to arrive; slow feedback, or sometimes none at all.

- **Business letters** are still one of a firm's main means of communication with the outside world. Letter-headed paper is used, which sometimes includes the firm's logo. There is a standard format for letters, which includes references, the date, the inside address, the salutation, the text of the letter and the close. They are useful for:

  - contracts

  - sending the same letter to a large number of people

  - answering queries

  - explaining complex matters which it would be difficult for the receiver to understand immediately

  - dealing with any matters where it is important that a written record should be kept

  - occasional formal occasions within the firm, such as invitations, notices of promotion, dismissals, etc.

12.5 *Layout of a business letter*

Letterhead includes writer's address	**Lovely Moves**
	12 Wilton Way
	Worrall
	Southshire
	Telephone: 01234 667459
Reference	WP/WH
Date	Today's date
Recipient's address	Mrs J Brown
	11 High Road
	Worrall
	Southshire
Salutation	Dear Mrs Brown
Text of letter	
Close	Yours sincerely
	Winston Powell

QUESTION SPOTTER

Exam questions might be set on the following:
▸ What are the names of two kinds of business forms?
▸ Why do companies hold an annual general meeting for shareholders?

■ **Annual report and accounts.** By law, companies must send a copy of their annual report and accounts to all shareholders.

■ **Business forms.** A variety of forms are used for routine messages. Using pre-printed forms ensures that no relevant information is omitted. Many of them are trading documents. Some of the main ones are:

- **quotations** by a firm for supply of goods or services

- **delivery notes**, which are delivered with the goods and signed by the customer to show they have been received

- **invoices**, which give details of the goods and show the amount of money owed

- **credit notes**, which are sent when a customer has been overcharged or faulty goods have been returned

- **statements of account** sent to regular customers every month giving details of transactions and the amount owed

ELECTRONIC MESSAGES

■ Advantages: Speed; accuracy; quick or instant feedback; message is usually – or can be – recorded.

■ Disadvantages: Expensive; whole systems sometimes crash.

■ **Mobile phones** allow users to make calls from most locations, indoors and outdoors. The messages are transmitted by radio beacons.

■ **Video conferences** allow business people to talk to colleagues in any part of the world. Special cameras and software are used to transmit words and images to computer screens or visual display units.

■ A **fax**, or facsimile, machine can send an exact copy of a document to another fax machine anywhere in the world. The sender puts the document in a fax machine, dials the fax number of the person or organization, and the fax machine at the other end prints a copy of the document automatically. Letters, plans, diagrams and drawings can all be transmitted in this way.

■ **Personal computers (PCs)** and **notebooks** – lightweight, portable computers – have revolutionized external communication, too. Work that used to involve a lot of people can now all be done by a few computer operators in each firm. Space is also saved, as all the records can be stored in the computer files instead of in large filing cabinets. Standard business letters, mail 'shots' to thousands of customers, letters to selected customers using a database, and many other communications can now be made far more easily and quickly.

■ By using a **modem**, messages can be sent along the telephone lines. This enables the computer to become part of a **WAN**, a **wide area network**, which links it to other computers anywhere in the world.

⊞ The Internet

- The **Internet**, which links millions of computer users, is the most rapidly growing means of global communication.

- The Internet provides an **electronic mail**, or **e-mail**, service to other users all over the world, which is much quicker and cheaper than the traditional postal service. The service provider stores the message in an electronic mail box until the receiver views it.

- In addition there are also millions of '**sites**', or pages, on the **World Wide Web (WWW)**, which provide information in words and pictures on almost every conceivable topic. Using a software **browser**, computer users can 'surf' the Net from site to site all over the world.

QUESTION SPOTTER

Exam questions might be set on the following:
▸ What are the advantages of e-mails?
▸ How has the Internet changed business communication?
▸ Describe one method of communication that a company might use with
  a) employees;
  b) shareholders;
  c) customers.

? CHECK YOURSELF QUESTIONS

Q1 What is the standard format for a report?

Q2 Explain when you would use:

  a a business form
  b a business letter

Q3 Which means of communication would you choose if you wanted to:

  a send a document that was wanted immediately in another country?

  b persuade another person to do something?

  c talk to a group of colleagues in a subsidiary company in the north of England?

  d examine something in great detail and make some recommendations?

  e give an order to a large number of people?

  f find some information that you have not found elsewhere?

  g explain your department's plans for the next year to a group of colleagues?

Answers are on page 172.

IT in manufacturing

⊞ Computer-assisted design

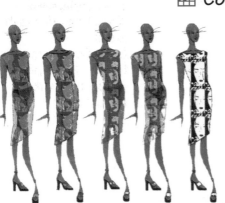

- **Computer-assisted design (CAD)** has completely changed the way in which many goods are created and developed. Using suitable software, a three-dimensional image of the product can be shown in colour on the screen of the **visual display unit (VDU)**. Its shape, composition and colour can be instantly altered or modified.

- The computer can show how the product would respond to the use of different materials in different conditions. It can calculate areas, weights, heights and other features of each design automatically.

- CAD can be used for designing objects of any size. An architect designing a new suspension bridge could show how it would react to different loads and different forces of wind. CAD would be just as useful for a designer creating a dress and the effects of using different weights of cloth, styles and colours.

13.1 *Designs by CAD: dress design in different fabrics (top) and telephone pods (bottom).*

⊞ Computer-aided manufacturing

- **Computer-aided manufacturing (CAM)** enables the product to be made direct from the display on the computer screen. For example, a chair could be designed on a computer screen. The instructions to make it could then be passed to a computer-controlled machine that cuts out the wooden chair frames, to another machine that cuts out the foam rubber for the cushion, and to another machine that cuts the material for the cushion covers. The chairs would then only have to be assembled.

- Computer-controlled machines are quick and easy to reset. It is therefore very easy to change the design and to instruct the machines to make a different version of the chair.

- In **flexible batch production** of this kind, smaller quantities of different versions of the same basic product can be produced with little loss of time.

⊞ Computer-integrated manufacturing

- **Computer-integrated manufacturing (CIM)** combines CAD and CAM in one integrated process, which extends from the initial design of the product and its components through all stages of its manufacture, including quality control, to the final delivery of finished goods from the factory using a computer-controlled system of distribution.

- Some of the most up-to-date examples of CIM are found in car factories. Dealers' orders for a car of a particular model, colour and engine size with any number of optional extras are fed into a central computer. It then sends instructions to satellite computers at individual workstations on the assembly line. The machines used in manufacturing are reprogrammed, or given new orders, while they are still operating to produce the cars required.

- This **flexible manufacturing system (FMS)** makes it much easier and quicker to produce different versions of the same product on assembly lines.

QUESTION SPOTTER

Exam questions might be set on the following:
▸ Give examples of two different firms which might use CAD.
▸ Explain the advantages of CIM for a) the company; b) its shopfloor workers; c) its customers.

▦ The use of robots in production

- Robots are widely used in car manufacturing plants for a variety of tasks, including welding, painting, grinding and polishing.

- 'Sighted' robots, which can recognize components and parts by their shape, are also employed to load raw parts into computer-controlled apparatus, which machines, or finishes, them. Robots and driverless trucks transport components just-in-time to teams of workers on the assembly line. Assembly lines in many other kinds of factories have become more and more automated, with robots and computer-controlled machines replacing human labour.

- Industrial robots have significant advantages. They are cheaper than employing manual labour. They can work 24 hours a day. They can also be used in dangerous or unhealthy environments, such as at the bottom of the ocean or inside nuclear processing plants.

BENEFITS AND DRAWBACKS OF AUTOMATION
- The main advantages of automation are:
  - great increase in output
  - increased productivity
  - higher-quality products
  - greater variety of mass-produced goods
- The main disadvantages are:
  - enormous capital cost
  - loss of jobs

? CHECK YOURSELF QUESTIONS

Q1 What is the difference between CAD and CAM?

Q2 State two advantages of using robots.

Answers are on page 172.

Distribution and IT

⊞ How has IT affected distribution?

- The impact of information technology has been no less dramatic on distribution. Manufacturers of well-known branded consumer goods and multiple retailers have set up huge state-of-the-art **distribution centres**, where goods are despatched to retailers **just-in-time** with as little human intervention as possible.

- **Bar codes** are attached to the boxes or wooden pallets holding goods as soon as they arrive from the factory. Hand-held **radio-frequency terminals** or long-range **scanners** are used to locate them in the warehouse. This means that forklift drivers do not have to leave their vehicles to find and load the required goods.

- Other distribution centres are even more highly automated. Computer-controlled automatic shelf loaders with long mechanical arms move up and down, and from left to right, along the range of warehouse shelves stacking or retrieving the goods.

- Packers no longer have to read the order from a printed list when they are putting a mixture of goods into the delivery boxes. To speed up the process, paperless **picking systems** are used.

⊞ How IT helps retailers

- Supermarkets pioneered many of these methods of distribution. At one time, batches of goods were delivered to stores in response to written orders. This batch-supply system has been replaced by an electronic-flow system, which delivers stock to each store just before it runs out.

- The system is completely automatic. As each item is sold in a supermarket store, the checkout assistant places its bar code in front of the scanning window of the **electronic point-of-sale (EPOS)** terminal.

- When the stock of any item starts to run out, new supplies are automatically ordered just-in-time from the supermarket's regional distribution centre by **electronic data interchange (EDI)** between computers, without any human intervention. The stock is delivered to the store once or twice a day, or with bigger stores even more frequently.

- Similar systems are also used by other big multiple retailers. The sales data recorded by the computer can be used in many other ways. Managers at the company's headquarters can use it to check on each store's sales and profitability. They can also use it to phase in re-orders of goods from the group's suppliers.

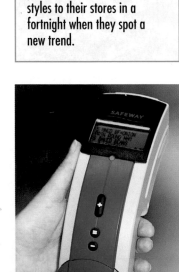

13.2 *Safeway's 'intelligent' hand-held scanner*

▦ IT in the financial sector

- Information technology has also had a great impact on the whole financial sector. Financial institutions in all parts of the world are linked together electronically, giving immediate access to each other.

- Most dealing in stocks and shares is no longer done face to face in Stock Exchanges, but on computer screens. Dealing goes on for 24 hours a day, sometimes automatically, with dealers' computers programmed to buy or sell when share prices are at a certain price.

USING PLASTIC CARDS
- Many financial transactions in high-street banks (and building societies) are carried out by electronic means using plastic **credit** and **debit cards**.

▦ Teleworking and the electronic office

- Information technology, with its widespread use of PCs and portable notebooks, word-processing, database and spreadsheet software, LANs, faxes, mobile phones, modems and e-mail, has completely revolutionized the modern office. These developments opened the way to **teleworking**, or working at home, using computers, phones, faxes and e-mail to maintain contact with company headquarters.

- Teleworking reduces a firm's costs, as it does not have to provide so much expensive office accommodation. Surveys have shown that productivity also rises. Employees also benefit, as they are freed from commuting problems and can work at their own pace.

- There are also disadvantages. Teleworkers miss the social contacts of office life and friendships with fellow workers.

▦ Effects of the IT revolution

- We are only at the beginning of the information technology revolution. Hundreds of IT applications have already been introduced, and many more are still being developed. They range from the use of **electronic tags** in crime prevention to **home shopping** through the Internet and **radar beams** linked to car computers to help reduce road accidents.

QUESTION SPOTTER

Exam questions might be set on the following:
▸ What is teleworking? What is one advantage for a) employers; b) staff?
▸ Describe the effects of information technology on share dealing.

■ IT has already had many major effects on business, including:

- greater productivity, as computer-controlled machines can work more quickly and more accurately than human beings and for longer periods of time

- greater flexibility among employees; all employees need to perform many more tasks, and managers need new skills

- increased redundancies among factory workers, office and shop workers and middle managers as a result of automation

- retraining for the redundant, and more training for workers to do highly skilled jobs

- more capital investment in information technology throughout the world

- more global competition through the increase in the speed of telecommunications and the greater amount of information available

CHECK YOURSELF QUESTIONS

Q1 What is electronic data interchange?

Q2 A multiple retailer of men's clothes has introduced an EPOS system. Describe the main advantages.

Answers are on page 173.

UNIT 14: GOVERNMENT INFLUENCE

Government policy

⊞ The government's fiscal policy

■ The government has a great influence over the whole economy through its fiscal policy. This consists of:

- the government's own spending
- direct and indirect taxation

⊞ Government spending and its effects

■ Apart from consumers, the government is easily the biggest spender in the country. Its total expenditure on such items as education, health, welfare, roads, defence and other items is currently about £370 billion a year.

■ If the government decided to increase its total spending by ten per cent – or £37 billion a year – there would be a great boost to the whole economy. More schools, roads and hospitals, naval vessels and military aircraft would be built, providing new jobs for millions of people. The boom, however, would be only brief.

■ The government gets much of its revenue, or income, from the taxes paid by individuals and businesses. These would certainly go up as more people would be working and spending more; but they would not go up fast enough to cover the massive increase in spending.

PUBLIC SECTOR BORROWING REQUIREMENT

■ Therefore, the government would have to borrow money for its huge **public sector borrowing requirement (PSBR)** so that its expenditure and its revenue balanced (see below).

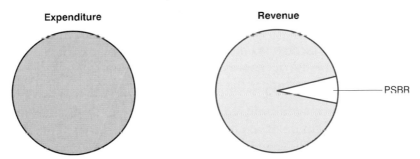

14.1 *Expenditure and revenue*

■ The government would have to start paying interest on its huge PSBR. It would have to increase taxes by massive amounts to pay the interest, or cut its spending drastically, or go even further into debt.

■ To avoid such problems, most governments keep a firm rein on **public spending**, or the amount they spend. To reduce uncertainty about public spending, the Labour government introduced a **comprehensive spending review** in 1998. This set out the spending plans of all government departments for the next three years.

QUESTION SPOTTER

Exam questions might be set on the following:
▶ Who are the biggest spenders in the national economy?
▶ Describe the likely effects of an increase in government spending on a) the government's own finances; b) the private sector; c) the public.

⊞ Taxation and its effects

- The government uses two main kinds of taxes:

   1 **Direct taxes**, such as income tax, are levied on people or businesses. People who earn more pay more income tax.

   2 **Indirect taxes**, such as the **duty** (or tax) on alcohol, are levied on goods and services. Everyone pays the same amount of tax according to the amount they buy.

- In general, any increase in tax will slow down business activity in some way, while a reduction in tax will tend to increase economic activity.

- Some of the main taxes are shown in Figure 14.2.

14.2 *Direct and indirect taxes*

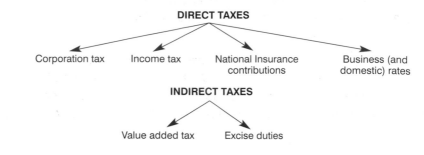

CORPORATION TAX

- **Corporation tax** is a direct tax charged on the profits of all private and limited companies. They can claim a number of allowances, which reduces the amount of tax they have to pay.

- A rise in corporation tax might force companies to reduce investment, pay lower dividends or cut costs. A reduction would allow companies to increase investment, put up dividends or pay higher wages.

INCOME TAX

- **Income tax** is also a direct tax, which is charged on the profits of sole proprietors and partnerships, and on private individuals who have incomes high enough to make them liable for tax.

- Employers deduct income tax directly from employees' pay before they receive it under the **PAYE (pay–as–you–earn)** system. Business people calculate their own tax under the self-assessment system.

- An increase in income tax will reduce the amount that consumers have to spend, while a cut in income tax will give them more money to save or spend.

NATIONAL INSURANCE CONTRIBUTIONS

- **National Insurance contributions (NICs)** go towards the costs of the state pension, the health service and welfare benefits. The employer deducts NICs directly from employees' pay and also makes a contribution for each employee.

- A rise in NICs would reduce consumer spending as employees would have less to spend. It would also increase firms' costs – and possibly force them to cut their other spending – as their NICs would also rise.

UNIFORM BUSINESS RATE

- The **uniform business rate** is applied at the same rate to businesses throughout the country. The amount is based on the rent that could be charged if the property was let.

- As the rate is based on the size and value of the property, any increase might force a business to move to smaller premises or put up its prices.

VALUE ADDED TAX (VAT)

- **Value added tax (VAT)** is the main indirect tax in Britain, producing as much revenue for the government as National Insurance contributions. It has to be paid on most goods and services. The standard rate is 17.5 per cent. Some goods are zero-rated, including most food and drink, books and newspapers, children's clothes and footwear. VAT was imposed at a lower rate on electricity and gas in 1994.

OTHER TAXES

- The government puts a number of other taxes on various goods and services. These include **excise duties** on alcohol, tobacco and petrol, which are collected by the Customs and Excise. There are also other taxes such as stamp duty on buying houses and shares, and road tax.

⊞ Control over interest rates

- Until 1997, the government was in charge of **monetary policy** as well as fiscal policy. Monetary policy controls the price that people and businesses have to pay for borrowing money, or the **interest rate**.

- One of the first acts of the Labour government, when it came to power in 1997, was to hand over control of interest rates to the monetary policy committee of the **Bank of England**. When the Bank changes the interest rate, the high-street banks and other lenders change their base rate to more or less the same level as the Bank's.

- The Bank makes its decision on purely economic grounds. Its main aim is to control **inflation**, which is a continuing rise in the general level of prices. If the Bank puts up interest rates, the whole economy will slow down because demand will fall. Prices, therefore, will also start to fall.

- However, the economy also slows down, so that unemployment may start to increase. The higher interest rate will also cause the value of the pound to rise. This will make British goods dearer in foreign countries, so it may be more difficult for manufacturers to sell their goods abroad.

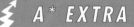

A* EXTRA

VAT is paid at every stage of production, but firms pay VAT only on the value added by their own work. If a manufacturing firm paid £2 for the raw material in a product which it then sold to a retailer for £3, it would pay tax only on the difference between the two prices, i.e. £1. Consumers cannot claim back the VAT they pay, because they add no value to the product.

QUESTION SPOTTER

Exam questions might be set on the following:
- State two kinds of taxes paid by a) consumers; b) companies.
- Explain why consumers pay most value added tax.

❓ CHECK YOURSELF QUESTIONS

Q1 a Who controls interest rates?

b What is inflation?

c How does a rise in interest rates help to cut inflation?

Q2 If a business borrowed £150,000 to buy a fleet of cars, and the bank put up its interest rates from 9.7 to 10.5 per cent, how much more would the business have to pay in interest in a year?

Answers are on page 173.

Government restraints

⊞ Controlling monopolies

■ As the first part of the unit has shown, any increase in taxes (or a rise in interest rates) can restrict general business activity. The government also restrains individual businesses in other ways by ensuring that one firm does not gain too much control over any market.

■ A **monopoly** exists when one firm has total control over the production of one kind of good or service, so that it can set the price it chooses for its products because there is no competition.

■ The government may investigate any merger that would create a market share of 25 per cent or more, or involve the acquisition of more than £70 million worth of assets. The investigation is carried out by the Director General of the **Office of Fair Trading** or the **Competition Commission**.

⊞ Regulation of privatized utilities

■ The utilities supply essential services, such as water, gas, electricity and telecommunications.

■ Although some competition has been introduced, the privatized companies are still very powerful. Therefore, the government has created special **regulators**, or watchdogs. The regulators have powers to control utilities' prices. The government can introduce a special **windfall tax** if it believes their profits are still too high.

⊞ Consumer protection

■ Consumers need special protection against utilities and other big, powerful companies because they are in a much weaker position.

■ Successive governments have passed a large number of laws to protect consumers. Some of the most important are the Sale of Goods Acts, the Trade Descriptions Acts, and the Consumer Credit Act.

■ The **Sale and Supply of Goods Act** of 1994 states that goods must be of 'satisfactory quality'. This means that they have to be:

- safe

- durable, or not likely to wear out quickly

- fit for all the purposes for which they are normally used

- free from minor defects, which includes their finish and appearance

■ These conditions also apply to sales goods, unless defects are pointed out at the time.

■ The **Trade Descriptions Act** of 1972 prohibits businesses from giving false or misleading descriptions of goods or services.

■ If either of these laws have been broken, the businesses must offer to repair or replace the goods or give a refund

- The **Consumer Credit Act** of 1974 gives greater protection to consumers when they borrow money or buy on credit. The Act:

  - introduced **licences** for firms who give credit

  - forced firms offering credit to state the **annual percentage rate** of interest, or APR

  - prevented firms inviting people under 18 to borrow money or to buy on credit

  - gave a **cooling–off period** of several days, or time to think, for people who signed credit agreements at home

  - restricted brokers' charges for mortgage offers that were not taken up

QUESTION SPOTTER

Exam questions might be set on the following:
- Which officials are responsible for seeing that laws protecting shoppers are carried out?
- Which Act of Parliament stops businesses giving false descriptions of goods?
- Explain the main provisions of the Sale and Supply of Goods Act 1994.

Enforcing consumer laws

- There are a number of official, and unofficial, bodies which try to ensure that these laws are enforced. In addition to investigating monopolies and restrictive trading, the Office of Fair Trading also looks after consumers' interests. It provides consumers with information about their rights. In serious cases, it will contact the firm concerned, or prosecute it.

TRADING STANDARDS OFFICERS

- **Trading Standards Officers**, employed by county councils, play a big part in enforcing the 50 Acts of Parliament and 500 sets of regulations that control the buying and selling of goods and services. They visit shops regularly, and if the laws have not been observed, the Trading Standards Officers may warn the businesses, or, in serious cases, prosecute them.

OMBUDSMEN

- The National Health Service (NHS) and local government have appointed **ombudsmen**, official investigators, to look into complaints by members of the public. In the private sector, banks, building societies and insurance companies have all set up their own ombudsman schemes.

UNOFFICIAL WATCHDOGS

- There are also a number of unofficial organizations that seek to protect consumers' rights. One of the most powerful is the **Consumers' Association**. It investigates all kinds of goods and services, and many other consumer issues, and publishes the results in the *Which?* series of magazines.

- **Citizens' Advice Bureaux** (CAB) provide general help and advice for consumers, and specific advice on a large range of topics.

14.3 Which? *magazine, published by the Consumers' Association*

CHECK YOURSELF QUESTIONS

Q1 a What is a monopoly situation?

   b Who would investigate it?

   c What action could be taken?

Q2 State two requirements of the Consumer Credit Act.

Answers are on page 173.

Government aid to business

⊞ How can the government help businesses?

■ The government also helps business in many ways. One of the most important is keeping its own expenditure as low as possible so that the private sector does not have to pay excessive taxes to support an inefficient public sector.

■ With varying success, it tries to create a good **infrastructure**, or physical environment of roads, railways, electricity supplies, etc., which makes it easy for businesses to operate.

■ It can encourage businesses to operate profitably, for example by reducing corporation tax or by giving large capital allowances to businesses that invest in new plant and machinery or training.

■ It can also provide special aid for particular problems. For the last 25 years or so, unemployment has been one of the main problems in Britain. Successive governments have encouraged businesses to help solve this problem by giving them special assistance if they create jobs in run-down areas of high unemployment. Some of the major government schemes are:

- urban development corporations

- enterprise zones

- regional assistance

URBAN DEVELOPMENT CORPORATIONS

■ In the 1980s, the government set up twelve **urban development corporations (UDCs)** to improve some inner-city areas. The infrastructure – roads, public buildings, leisure facilities, etc. – was modernized in the hope that the private sector would open businesses. The first two UDCs were set up in Merseyside and London Docklands in 1981. The London Docklands Development Corporation (LDDC), with its Canary Wharf scheme, has been an outstanding success.

■ Other UDCs were established in Birmingham, Bristol, Leeds, Manchester, Plymouth, Sheffield, Teeside and Tyne and Wear.

14.4 *Canary Wharf before and after redevelopment*

ENTERPRISE ZONES

■ Twenty-four **enterprise zones** were also set up to attract firms to inner-city areas. These are small areas of inner cities with high levels of unemployment. New businesses that set up in the enterprise zone, or established firms that move there, receive a number of benefits. These include:

- exemption from, or a lower level of, business rates

- 100 per cent tax allowances for new buildings

- easier planning permission

■ The enterprise zone lasts for ten years, but it can be extended.

REGIONAL ASSISTANCE

- Some areas of the country suffer particularly from high rates of unemployment, lack of opportunities and general neglect. These are called **assisted areas**. There are four main kinds (see Figure 14.5):

  - development areas, which need most help

  - split development/intermediate areas, which need a large amount of help

  - intermediate areas, which need some help

  - split intermediate/non-assisted areas, which need least help

- Northern Ireland has its own assistance schemes. Grants or loans are given to businesses that are likely to grow over a number of years.

- The government gives businesses **regional selective assistance** if they create new jobs in these areas. Grants are given to both manufacturing and service industries. However, the firms have to prove that they really need the money and would not create the jobs without the grant.

- The government tries to attract **foreign firms** to assisted areas by giving them large grants if they open factories and other businesses in areas of high unemployment.

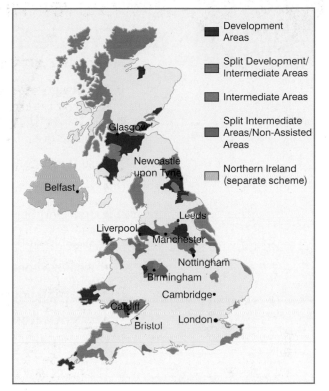

■	Development Areas
■	Split Development/ Intermediate Areas
■	Intermediate Areas
■	Split Intermediate Areas/Non-Assisted Areas
☐	Northern Ireland (separate scheme)

14.5 *Assisted areas in the UK Source: COI, Britain: An Official Handbook*

A* EXTRA

Britain continues to attract more foreign firms than any other member country of the European Union. In the year ended in March 2000, there were over 750 new inward investments creating over 52,000 jobs. The main attractions are the skilled workforce, the English language, which is the main international language, and the weaker labour laws protecting workers.

CHECK YOURSELF QUESTIONS

Q1 a What is an enterprise zone?

   b State one benefit for firms which set up business there.

Q2 a Which kind of assisted area receives the most aid?

   b Look at Figure 14.5. Name one area of this kind.

Answers are on page 174.

UNIT 15: SOCIAL RESPONSIBILITIES

Choosing a business location

▦ What factors influence the choice of location?

- The factors that may influence a company in choosing a location for its business are:

  - suitability of sites and premises

  - nearness to market/suppliers

  - transport links and communications

  - suitable workforce

  - local environment

  - local authorities

  - external economies of scale

  - government grants and other benefits (see pages 132–133)

- It is never easy to choose the best **business location**. Businesses have to consider each factor thoroughly and find the most favourable combination.

▦ Finding suitable sites and premises

- Businesses have a choice of four main kinds of site, all of which are very different. They are:

  - city centres and suburbs

  - out-of-town developments

  - industrial estates

  - greenfield sites

CITY CENTRES AND SUBURBS

- Most retailers have to choose between the first two options – city centres/suburbs and out-of-town developments – because that is where most consumers shop. Premises cost less to buy or rent in side streets off the high street and in the suburbs of a city, but the number of shoppers also declines.

- City premises sometimes cost a large amount of money to refit and refurbish. It is also sometimes difficult to obtain planning permission for change of use.

- Parking restrictions, plus general traffic congestion, cause some of the biggest problems for retailers in towns and cities. There is also usually much more competition than there is on small, out-of-town developments.

> ### ⚡ A* EXTRA
>
> High streets, which were in serious decline, are fighting back against their out-of-town rivals with more covered shopping malls and arcades, and a new range of leisure retail outlets, including restaurants, coffee shops, novelty shops, etc.

OUT-OF-TOWN DEVELOPMENTS

- There are three main kinds of **out-of-town development**:
  - small, mixed retail and office developments
  - very large shopping centres, like the Metro Centre at Gateshead
  - factory outlets selling mainly reduced-price goods
- The main advantages for retailers are:
  - cheaper rents than in city centres
  - purpose-built premises
  - more room for expansion
  - easier parking
  - large number of consumers dedicated to buying
- On small developments, there is the additional advantage of less competition. For example, there is often only one supermarket or one DIY store or one furniture store.
- However, most sole proprietors would find it impossible to move to out-of-town sites, as there are often no small premises at rents they could afford.

INDUSTRIAL ESTATES

- There are sometimes a few retailers on **industrial estates**, such as a stationery and photocopying firm supplying other businesses.
- Industrial estates are more suitable for manufacturers. The main advantages are:
  - purpose-built units
  - room for expansion
  - easy parking
  - large turning areas for articulated lorries
  - relaxed planning permission
  - less chance of complaints from residents about noise, pollution, etc.

GREENFIELD SITES

- These sites have all the benefits of industrial estates, plus the added advantage of creating a completely new, purpose-built plant that is appropriate for the business concerned.
- Companies often choose greenfield sites in assisted areas so that they get the additional benefit of government grants.

15.1 *A purpose-built industrial plant on a greenfield site*

⊞ Means of acquiring premises

- Businesses often have to make a further choice with premises, as they can either buy the freehold of the premises or rent it on lease for a number of years.

- To buy the premises, the business has to invest a large amount of money or take out a large mortgage for twenty or thirty years. However, commercial property usually increases in value over the years, so that it may well become a valuable business asset.

- If a company rents a property on lease, it only has to pay a relatively small sum of money for the lease. However, it has to pay rent every year and never acquires a stake in the property. Moreover, the value of its lease will decline over the years until it is worth practically nothing just before the lease ends.

⊞ Nearness to market and suppliers

- At one time, some firms, such as steel and textile manufacturers, which relied on coal for power and raw materials from overseas, had to be near coal mines and ports. But improved transport has given manufacturers a much wider choice of location.

- However, if a manufacturer's raw materials are extremely large and heavy, it may still be worthwhile for the manufacturer to choose a location near their source; or if it sells huge machinery or equipment, it might be useful for the manufacturer to be located near the places where they are used.

- Most retailers need to be near their main markets. Many suppliers need to be within easy reach of the firms they supply, particularly if just-in-time is used.

⊞ Transport links and communications

- Improved transport has probably been the biggest factor in increasing the choice of business location. Over 80 per cent of goods in Britain are delivered by road, which is a far more flexible means of transport than either rail or water.

- Except for local businesses and some service industries, access to motorways is of major importance to most manufacturers, wholesalers and suppliers.

RAIL FREIGHT

- Until recently, most exports to Europe also went by road. However, the Channel Tunnel has speeded up journeys to the Continent so much that railways may regain a bigger share of the market.

- There are seven other Eurocentral rail terminals – in Birmingham, Liverpool, Manchester, Wakefield, Daventry, Doncaster and Willesden in London – so these could become popular areas for exporters to Europe.

15.2 *Most goods in Britain are delivered by road*

COMMUNICATIONS

- Recent progress in information technology has made it much easier for many companies in the services sector to conduct their business by phone and other electronic means. This enables the companies to locate in remote areas of the country where wages tend to be cheaper. Huge **call centres**, where telephonists take calls from customers, are one of the fastest-growing sectors in the economy.

Obtaining a suitable workforce

- A business has to consider whether a suitable supply of labour of all types is available in the area.

- Local wage rates are also an important factor. The differences in wages between various parts of the country are less than they were, but they still exist.

The local environment

- The local environment is also important. If the location is pleasant and has good facilities, it will be much easier to attract and retain employees – and their families. This is a particularly important factor when an existing business is relocating to another area.

- Some of the desirable features are:

  - plenty of good housing at reasonable prices and of different grades, from terraced house and 'semis' to executive homes

  - good schools, both state and private; colleges that can provide training for employees; and universities that might provide help with research

  - good sport and entertainment facilities, such as swimming pools, fitness centres, golf courses, cinemas, theatres and clubs

  - attractive countryside within easy access

  - a good road system and efficient public transport

- The local environment is also important for retailers in a different way. If it is shabby and unattractive, it will not attract customers.

ATTITUDES OF LOCAL AUTHORITY

- The attitudes of local authorities towards business are still important.

- It is often much easier for a business to obtain planning permission if it can show that the development will create new jobs. In some assisted areas, local authorities offer financial inducements for businesses to move to the area.

QUESTION SPOTTER

Exam questions might be set on the following:
- ▸ What percentage of goods are delivered by road?
- ▸ What kind of manufacturers need to be near a port?
- ▸ Why do suppliers of automobile parts locate near car manufacturers' plants?

⊞ External economies of scale

- Firms in the same kind of business often set up in the same area. Lawyers are often found in the same street; restaurants in the same part of a town or a city; car factories in the same region, such as the West Midlands.

BENEFITS FOR BUSINESS

- By being close to one another, businesses of the same kind gain great external economies of scale. For example, restaurants will be able to obtain supplies of food and wine, and customers, more easily. Local bank managers may be more helpful, as they will understand restaurants' special financial needs – and problems.

- Eventually, if the restaurant area becomes big enough, a local college may start catering courses, which would provide a source of recruits and part-time workers for the restaurants. Or a specialized job agency may be opened.

- There are many other examples of external economies. For instance, a university may carry out research for a local industry; trade associations may provide training courses for all member firms.

- External economies of scale provide benefits for a whole group of firms, unlike economies of scale which benefit individual firms (see Unit 3).

QUESTION SPOTTER

Exam questions might be set on the following:
- ▸ State two external economies of scale.
- ▸ Name three features which would make a town attractive for businesses.
- ▸ Describe some of the main problems that businesses might find if they moved to a different area of the country.

? CHECK YOURSELF QUESTIONS

Q1 Name three factors that are important in deciding where to locate a business and give one example of each.

Q2 Karen, who was a buyer in a large department store, is going to open an shop selling young children's clothes. For the last few weeks, she has been looking at premises in various parts of the city. She has made the following notes on the two shops that might be suitable.

Study the notes on the right and then answer the following questions:

a Which factors involving the location of a business are referred to in the notes about Shop A and Shop B?

b What other factors might be relevant in both cases?

c Taking only the factors described in the notes, state which shop seems to be the most suitable.

Rent £4,000 a year. Business Rates £1,200 a year. Will need total shop-fitting. (Cost £13,500?) Yellow lines. Passers-by - mainly office workers and older residents. Nearest high street half a mile away. Street a bit dingy. Facing park with children's playground. Few other shops, two of them closes. Several pubs.

High street a couple of blocks away. One-hour parking meters. Shop will need a little redecorating. Two schools nearby. Rent £9,000 a year. Business rates £2,700 a year. In a row of up market shops, delicatessens, wine shops etc. Quite smart floral window boxes. Not many passers-by. Perhaps more of an evening trade.

Answers are on page 174.

Social costs and benefits

⊞ What are social costs and benefits?

- When a company chooses a location for its business, it is concerned almost entirely with the **private costs** – such as the rent or purchase price of the premises, the level of wages in the area – and the **private benefits** – such as the chance of making large profits or increasing market share. The **social costs** – the adverse effects on other people in the locality or on the nation as a whole – and the **social benefits** – the advantages for the rest of society – are far less important.

DIFFERING USES OF THESE BUSINESS TERMS

- It is most important to remember that these business terms – social costs and social benefits – are used in differing ways. Sometimes they are used separately from private costs and private benefits, as they are in the section above. Sometimes, however, they are combined. In this case, the term 'social costs' includes *all* the effects on both the business itself (private costs) and on the rest of society (external costs).

- Social benefits are treated in the same way.

- If the terms are being used in this way,
  - social costs = private costs + external costs
  - social benefits = private benefits + external benefits

- If nothing is stated or implied in the exam question, you should include both the private and external aspects in your answer.

- If it is clearly stated, or indicated, that only the external costs and benefits are needed in your answer, you should not include the private costs and benefits.

- However, if you do include the private costs and benefits by mistake, examiners will usually reward them, too. Therefore, if you are in doubt, it is better to include both kinds of costs and benefits in your answer.

⊞ Social costs and benefits of closing a factory

- When a big company closes an unprofitable factory that provides most of the jobs in a town, it is aware of the social costs of its action, but it usually puts its private benefits first.

- The company would argue that its primary duty is to its shareholders. Moreover, if it did not close the factory, some of its other factories, or even the whole company, might not survive, which would have even wider and more disastrous social costs.

- In closing the factory, the company would suffer some private costs, too: redundancy payments; reduction of capital; possible damage to company image. But the effects on the workforce, the local community and the country as a whole would be far greater.

⚡ A* EXTRA

All business actions have social costs and benefits. In recognition of this fact, some companies have introduced social audits which examine their performance in relation to equal rights, the environment and the community.

💡 QUESTION SPOTTER

- ▸ Give one example of a) a private cost, and b) a private benefit for an expanding business.
- ▸ Why do businesses need to consider external costs as well as private costs?
- ▸ Describe the social costs and benefits of a new football stadium.

- Many people in the town would lose their jobs. Shops, pubs, restaurants and many other kinds of firms would suffer. Local suppliers might have to make some of their workforce redundant, while others might be forced to close. Colleges and universities in the areas might lose students or research contracts. The factory closure could produce a 'ghost' town of unemployed.

- There would also be effects on the whole country. The government (i.e. the whole nation) would lose the benefit of the factory's corporation tax, and the employees' income tax and National Insurance contributions. The government would have to pay jobseekers' allowance and welfare benefits to the unemployed.

- Apart from the redundancy payments, the company makes no contribution to the social costs of closing the factory. But the reduction in private costs will send the company's profits soaring.

▦ Summary of social costs and benefits

- The effects of the company's action could be summarized as follows:

SOCIAL COSTS (I.E. PRIVATE COSTS + EXTERNAL COSTS)
- Private costs
  - redundancy payments to the workforce
  - loss of capital if the factory had to be sold for less than its purchase price
  - damage to company image if closure resulted in strikes
  - loss of key workers if they refused to relocate to other sites
- External costs
  - reduced income for workers and their families
  - social and economic impact on the rest of the town, e.g. loss of trade in shops, restaurants, pubs, etc.
  - loss of work for suppliers
  - increase in regional unemployment
  - Increased welfare benefits

SOCIAL BENEFITS (I.E. PRIVATE BENEFITS + EXTERNAL BENEFITS)
- Private benefits
  - reduced costs through closing factory
  - lower unit costs of production at other sites
  - greater profitability for the company as a whole
- External benefits
  - less traffic and noise near the factory
  - possibly more employment on sites in other parts of the country

⊞ Changing attitudes to business

- In recent years, business has been forced to become more aware of the social costs and benefits of its activities. This has been brought about largely by increasing public, scientific and governmental concern about the impact of business on society and the environment.

- The pressure has been so great that the government and the European Union have been forced to pass laws to protect the environment.

COMPANIES INTRODUCE ETHICAL POLICIES

- These environmental concerns have made companies more aware of the social effects of their actions. Many big companies have introduced an **ethical policy**, laying down rules of fair behaviour towards the rest of society. Some of the policies that might be covered are:

  - the **environment**, including reducing pollution, maintaining eco-systems, saving energy, disposing of waste safely

  - **health and safety**, not only in relation to the company's activities, but also to using new technology that might be harmful or unsafe

  - the **local community**, by sponsoring events for charities and providing help and special services for old people and people with special needs

  - the **wider world**, by trading fairly with developing countries, not exploiting cheap foreign labour and refusing to deal with countries that abuse human rights

THE INFLUENCE OF PRESSURE GROUPS

- Pressure groups have played a big part in changing attitudes. In recent years, the number of pressure groups has increased greatly. Some are international, like Greenpeace. Others are national, like the anti-smoking group ASH (Action on Smoking and Health). And many more are local, set up with the aim of reducing noise and smells from a local factory or installing road humps, or 'sleeping policemen', on a busy road.

⚡ A* EXTRA

Environmental pressure groups, such as Friends of the Earth, maintain that the global economy is responsible for a loss of natural habitats and biodiversity, and increasing inequality between the developed nations and the rest of the world.

💡 QUESTION SPOTTER

Exam questions might be set on the following:
- State one a) private cost; b) private benefit; c) external cost; d) external benefit of a new out-of-town superstore.
- Why do small businesses often support local charities?
- What impact do oil companies have upon the environment?

❓ CHECK YOURSELF QUESTIONS

Q1 Explain the term 'social costs' and give one example of each.

Q2 If a regional airport was extended so that it could be used by bigger jets, what would be the social costs and benefits for the locality?

Q3 What is a pressure group? Give one example.

Answers are on page 175.

Exam questions and student answers

Ten years ago, three brothers, who were all successful businessmen, formed a private company when they opened a small airport in the Midlands. They all had experience related to the aircraft industry: one as a finance director of a multinational company, the second as the head of a large manufacturing business producing parts for aircraft and the third as the proprietor of a travel agency.

The service they intended to offer mainly involved internal flights within the United Kingdom for businessmen, and weekend and holiday travellers.

Two years ago, the company, Midlands Flightpath, became a plc. The brothers are now planning to expand by building another runway and adding further customer facilities such as lounges and restaurants. They have also transferred their head office to the centre of the adjacent city.

I   Describe three tertiary industries which are likely to be involved in the expansion of the airport and how they will be affected.   12 marks

A tertiary industry is one which provides some kind of service to all the other industries and businesses and to the consumer. With the expansion of the tertiary areas of the economy, entrepreneurs have used their skills to develop new industries. In relation to the airport, these would include transport, distribution and financial services. Three tertiary industries which might be involved are: road transport, computer operators and banks.

Road transport provides a method of delivering goods and equipment from building materials to furnishings. There are also huge container lorries for delivering goods and materials. Road transport will be affected in the building of a new runway through the need to deliver all kinds of building materials, furniture and fittings, extra restaurant and canteen food and equipment and probably transport for new employees.

The new runway will also mean the expansion of the offices because there will be more business and planes using the airport. This is likely to require more computers and therefore computer operators. Firms providing business servers and computer networks are likely to benefit and they will sell more computer accessories and software. There may also be a demand for computer training for the new employees.

The building of a runway and the expansion of the airport will also have a multiplier effect on the area as a whole, because other tertiary businesses, such as banks, are likely to benefit with the increase in the number of workers, visitors and tourists to the airport.

10/12

⊞ How to score full marks

- This question would be level marked. This is how the examiner's marks scheme would be structured:

  - Level 1: Mention of three tertiary industries, and how they will be affected, showing a basic understanding of the topic.

    1–3 marks

  - Level 2: More specific linkage of the three industries with the expansion of the airport, showing a clear understanding of the topic.

    4–8 marks

  - Level 3: Detailed understanding, with full explanation of how the industries will be affected.

    9–12 marks

- There are two parts to this question: firstly, a description of the three tertiary industries, and secondly, how they will be affected. You must always ensure that you answer all parts of a question and, in this case, that you give them equal weight.

- There are many other examples of tertiary industries which the student could have selected, such as legal services, rail and air transport, retail services, insurance, mortgage lenders, any of which are of equal validity.

- This student has defined 'tertiary' and added an extra, relevant, comment about entrepreneurs. He/She has answered the question correctly by mentioning only the effects on the three industries involved and not on the owners of the airport.

- This answer falls within Level 3 of the mark scheme and scores ten marks out of a possible 12. To score the extra two marks, the student would need to have described in more detail how banks would have been affected. He/She did this for the first two examples of tertiary industries – road transport and computer operators – but not for banks.

2 a) Explain TWO factors which might have influenced
their decision to become a plc.

4 marks

> Two factors which may have influenced the company to become a plc are:
> – It would be easier to raise capital because the company could sell shares
>   on the stock exchange. When they were a private company, they would
>   have got their money from the smaller number of people who had
>   shares. On the stock exchange, anyone can buy shares, so if the
>   company seems successful many people will buy the shares.
> – It is also easier for a plc to borrow money from banks and other
>   financial institutions.

4/4

b) Describe TWO disadvantages to the directors through changing
from a private company to a plc.

4 marks

> Two disadvantages to the directors which may arise from changing
> ownership to a plc are:
> – They will have less control over the purchase of shares. When they were
>   a private limited company, only the other directors or approved people
>   could buy them. As a plc, anyone can buy their shares through the
>   stock exchange.
> – They will have less control over the running of the company because
>   the shareholders may be more interested in getting dividends than in
>   any aims the directors may have. The directors may wish to venture
>   into new areas of business, but the shareholders may think this is too
>   risky and vote against them.

4/4

▦ How to score full marks

- The answer to part a) is very good and scores full marks.

- The other advantage is that if the business is successful, the share prices will also rise, thus enhancing the value of the company without any further investment by the directors.

- The answer to part b) is also good. The student has read the question properly and dealt specifically with the disadvantages to the directors, as required, and not to the company as a whole. Two relevant aspects have been described which have gained the full four marks.

- Another disadvantage which candidates rarely seem to appreciate is that when the company was a private limited company, the directors and shareholders were one and the same. In a public limited company, most shares are owned by institutional investors. They buy thousands of shares and therefore have enormous influence over the way the company is run through their votes at annual general meetings. In some cases, they can even force the chairman or some directors to resign. So the original directors – and owners – of the company could find themselves replaced.

3 Describe the objectives the business may have had when the company was formed, and how they may have changed over the years.

12 marks

> In the early years, the first objective would have been to get the business going. This might mean at the beginning that they would only break even in order to survive. The next objective would have been to market the airport and to get more airlines and passengers to use their services. At the beginning, they would offer their services as cheaply as possible in order to get customers. They would then start to make a profit and their aim would be to gradually increase their profits and get more customers. Their business aims would change as they became successful. Their objectives would then be to expand the business. They would also be hoping to make more profit and the formation of a public company means that they hope to raise more capital.

6/12

How to score full marks

- This question would be level marked as follows:
  - Level 1: Mention of at least three objectives with simple explanation.

    1–3 marks
  - Level 2: Explanation of objectives and showing a clear understanding of likely changes.

    4 8 marks
  - Level 3: Detailed description of objectives, showing understanding of why they may have changed over the years.

    9–12 marks

- The student's answer reaches Level 2. The six marks awarded are for the points mentioned, but the answer does not warrant further marks because the student has failed to develop the points made. It is essential to do this in order to move into Level 3 of the mark scheme.

- To reach the top of Level 3, the answer would need to have developed each point in the following ways:
  - to define what is meant by 'to get the business going';
  - to explain 'break even' and why it is necessary. If a company can break even, it will be able to keep going over the short term, because although it is not making a profit, it will cover all its costs.
  - to give an indication of how the profits will be increased. This will be done either by improving the service or offering facilities superior to their competitors. The company must also have very clear aims about how it can expand.

- The student also needed to explain why customer satisfaction is a continuous necessity and how it can be retained. He/She has described expansion adequately, although he/she might have explained that growth is also dependent on an increase in market share.

4   a)   Explain how fixed and variable costs are sometimes confused.   4 marks

> It is sometimes difficult to tell the difference between fixed and variable
> costs, because fixed costs may sometimes vary and also variable costs
> may increase or decrease..   1/4

   b)   Give four examples of each which the business will have.   4 marks

> Four examples of fixed costs are salaries, mortgage repayments, rent,
> insurance.
> Four examples of variable costs are fuel, wages, raw materials, repairs.   4/4

▦ How to score full marks

- The answer to part a) is meaningless and does not attempt to address the question. No examples have been given.

- The student needs to show some way in which some costs may appear to be both fixed or variable. It would be sufficient to mention one point, if fully explained and developed.

- Examples might be:
  - Wages may be classified as a fixed cost, if staff are employed on a permanent basis. But if a member of staff works overtime, the extra expense would be a variable cost.

  - Telephone charges are composed of a standing charge, plus the charge for all phone calls. The standing charge is fixed, no matter how many calls are made, but the call charges will vary from one quarter to another.

  - Similarly, there is a standing electricity charge which must be paid regardless of how much electricity is used.

- This is a fairly standard question which frequently seems to confuse students. It would help you to have a few examples ready in your mind.

- The examples given in part b) are correct and score the full four marks.

---

5   Suggest four ways by which Midlands Flightpath might raise money to finance its expansion.   8 marks

> Four ways it might raise the money would be: bank loan, overdraft, issue of
> more shares, sale of assets.   4/8

▦ How to score full marks

- The student gains one mark for each correct statement, but the fact that there are eight marks available should have told him/her that an explanation of each statement is required:

  - A bank loan may be the best solution, because the company will repay the loan over a number of years.

  - An overdraft may be attractive, as the company would have to pay interest only on the amount owing at any time. But interest rates may vary, and the bank may prefer the company to have a loan.

  - A special share issue would raise more capital in the long term, but it is a less immediate and certain method of raising instant finance.

  - The sale of assets is possible if the company has equipment or buildings which are disposable, but in a situation of expansion, there may be few available.

- Hire purchase, leasing or extended credit terms would also be suitable methods for raising part of the money.

- When answering questions of this kind, with a number of alternatives, it is important that you select the most suitable or likely points.

6 This is part of the balance sheet of Midlands Flightpath for the year ending 2001/2002.

	£ million
Current assets	
Debtors	503.3
Investments	114.4
Cash in hand and at bank	62.4
	680.1
Creditors: amounts falling due within one year	
Loans	45.9
Corporation tax	60.7
Dividend	18.6
Creditors	421.2
	546.4

a) Calculate the company's working capital, showing your workings.   4 marks

> Its working capital was £133.7 million.

2/4

b) Why is it important for the company to know its working capital?   4 marks

> It is most important for a company to be aware of its working capital at all times, because if its current liabilities exceeded its current assets, the company would be unable to pay its immediate debts. The company would, therefore, be insolvent.
> It would be forced to sell off some of its tangible assets or apply to its bankers for an immediate overdraft or loan, so that it acquired enough cash to pay its liabilities. If it had to sell off its tangible assets quickly, the company would almost certainly get a lower price than their real value.

4/4

⊞ How to score full marks

- The answer to part a) can score only two marks as it does not show the workings as requested.

- Working capital is calculated by deducting the current liabilities from the current assets. The workings, therefore, are £680.1 million − £546.4 million = £133.7 million.

- The answer to part b) is a very good answer which covers all the main points and deserves full marks.

7 Describe the methods of market research that Midlands Flightpath might have used before deciding to expand the airport. Suggest which methods they might employ.   12 marks

It would be necessary for Midlands Flightpath to make a list of the information they required to come to a decision. They would want to consider the current economic situation, the competition they faced from other airports, the potential customers, and market trends and developments.

The methods to be used would include desk research, both internal or external, and field research, involving contact with people or organizations. Desk research would involve reference to printed material in magazines, trade journals, reports and company balance sheets. This is external desk research, which would tell them about competitors, what the market was and what new developments were taking place. They could also use primary methods, such as interviewing their current list of customers and contacting companies using the airport facilities to ascertain their future plans. They could find out from passengers whether they would use overnight accommodation or whether they would like more secure parking. The current economic situation would tell them if business and investment was expanding or contracting.

The methods which would be most suitable for Midlands Flightpath would be mostly desk research because of the specialised services they are offering. It would also be necessary to know the prices being charged at other airports. Primary research would involve interviewing passengers to discover their needs and also any criticisms they may have.

10/12

▦ How to score full marks

- The student was not asked for definitions of the methods of market research, so the introductory sentences of the answer are therefore not relevant, even if correct.

- Make sure you read the question carefully so that you don't waste precious time providing information that you have not been asked for.

- The student does, however, gain marks for linking the purpose of external desk research with information about competitors and new developments. The answer generally is rather rambling but does contain some good detail, e.g. the specific aims of the questions to be answered by market research, such as the prices charged by competitors. He/She has also made specific suggestions of what to ask passengers, and this part of the answer is good.

- It is important when answering a question of this kind not merely to list the methods, but to explain why they are suitable in a particular instance.

- If this had been done rather better in this answer, then it would have scored the full 12 marks.

8 a) Write a job advertisement for a receptionist in the head office
of Midlands Flightpath. Outline the duties, experience necessary,
salary range, fringe benefits and any other necessary information.   10 marks

> RECEPTIONIST, full time, required for head office of Midlands
> Flightpath, an expanding airport in the Midlands. Front
> reception/office duties involve receiving visitors, making
> appointments, answering phone, dealing with complaints, using a
> computer, sending e-mail and fax messages. There is an entitlement to
> five weeks' holiday after one year, health insurance and child-care
> facilities. Attendance will be required for one Saturday in three,
> arranged with two other receptionists. Salary range £11,000 to £14,000
> according to experience.   8/10

b) Explain where would you place the advertisement and give your reasons.   4 marks

> I would place the advertisement in a local paper, as it is not the kind of
> job which would normally attract applicants from other parts of the
> country. A regional daily newspaper might be more suitable than a
> local weekly paper as it covers a greater area. The advertisement would
> be seen by a greater number of likely candidates.   3/4

▦ How to score full marks

- Part a) is a good answer, but rather too detailed.
- It is not necessary to state that receptionists receive visitors and answer the phone, as that is their normal function. However, the student is right to state that the applicant must have experience of computers, e-mails and faxes, as not all receptionists need this knowledge.
- The stated fringe benefits are sensible, although it must be remembered that there may also be male applicants who would be less likely to require child care.

- The salary range does not indicate whether there are any increments. The advertisement could have given some indication of the activities of the company and whether any knowledge of them is required.
- Part b) is also a good answer, with coherent reasons for the choice of media.
- The candidate should have stated that the advertisement should also be placed in Job Centres, where it might be seen by interested people who are actively looking for employment.

It had always been Jo Browne's ambition to run her own business. She had taken a course in retailing and accounting at her local college, and two years ago, she opened a children's clothes shop in Brighton. It was an immediate success, and after a few months, she had to take on two assistants. She bought a computer and office equipment and more display cases out of her profits. Six months later, she obtained a contract to supply school uniform for a small private school. She moved to larger premises and took on three more staff. Jo has decided that she does not wish to expand further because she wants the business to remain at a size where she can continue to run it herself. She will now concentrate on supplying uniforms for small schools in the area and good-quality clothes for young children.

1
a) Give two advantages which a sole trader enjoys. — 2 marks

b) Describe what you think is the main disadvantage a sole trader may suffer, apart from unlimited liability. — 4 marks

c) What is unlimited liability, and how does it affect a sole trader? — 3 marks

2
a) Compare Jo Browne's business objectives with those of a mass-market clothing retailer such as Littlewoods. — 6 marks

b) Explain three ways by which Jo can measure the success of her business. — 6 marks

3 Jo has decided that she needs a van for delivery of her orders. She intends to obtain one either by leasing or hire purchase.

a) Describe two characteristics of leasing and of hire purchase. — 4 marks

b) What method of obtaining the van would you recommend? State your reasons. — 3 marks

4
a) Which kind of market is Jo's business in? — 1 mark

b) Give one example of: — 6 marks
   i) a commodity market
   ii) an industrial market
   iii) a financial market
   iv) a consumer market
   v) a niche market
   vi) a traditional market

c) What is the difference between product-oriented goods and market-oriented goods? — 4 marks

d) Why have industrial markets become more market oriented? Give one example of an organizational market. — 6 marks

5 Jo Browne is thinking of setting up her own website on the Internet. Describe some of the benefits she might gain. — 8 marks

Answers and examiner's comments can be found on page 176.

Check Yourself Answers and Comments

UNIT 1: BUSINESS FUNDAMENTALS
1 Production (page 3)

Q1 Non-durable goods are used soon after they are bought, but durable goods last for a long time until they wear out or are replaced. Ice-cream is a non-durable good and a car is a durable good.

Comment In simple definition questions of this type, you are often asked to provide examples. It is therefore a good idea to remember one or two examples of the key terms that you learn. You must give a valid example to score full marks.

Q2a Capital is the stock of goods which a country uses to produce other goods and services. A factory is one example.

Comment Capital has this meaning in economics. Be careful not to confuse it with the different meaning in accounting, where it is the money that the owners have put into their business and which is shown on the balance sheet as capital (see Unit 5).

Q2b The process of extracting or growing raw materials which can then be used to make other goods. One example would be a farmer growing wheat.

Comment Again, you must be careful not to confuse 'production' and 'product'. Production is the process by which goods and services are made. Product is the goods or services that a business provides for its customers.

Q3 The percentage increase was 25%.

Comment Fifteen per cent is wrong. With questions of this type, you have to be careful not to confuse percentage points and percentage increase (or decrease). In this case, the number of employees in the services sector has risen by 15 percentage points, from 61 to 76 per cent. However, that is not the same as a percentage rise. That is calculated by dividing the increase in percentage points by the original percentage and multiplying by 100, i.e.
$\frac{15}{61} \times 100 = 24.59$
Therefore the correct answer (to the nearest whole number) is 25 per cent.

2 Production chains and markets (page 5)

Q1a An economy in which some resources are controlled and owned by private individuals, some by the State or by public authorities, and some by voluntary agencies. In other words, it contains private, public and voluntary sectors.

Comment Until recently, China, Russia and other countries in Eastern Europe had planned, or command, economies in which practically all economic activity was centrally controlled by the State. Russia and the Eastern European countries have introduced mixed economies, and China is also liberalising its economy.

Q1b i) private sector
ii) mainly in the public sector, though nurses are also employed in private hospitals and some are recruited for the public sector through private sector agencies

iii) voluntary sector
iv) private sector
v) all three sectors

Comment This question is not so simple as it may seem, as you need a good knowledge of what is currently happening in the business world to answer it correctly. You will score much higher marks in your exam if you show that you have some knowledge of what is happening in the real business world. Therefore, keep reading the financial and business sections of newspapers and listen to business programmes on the radio and watch any television features on business.

Q2 A market puts buyers and sellers in touch so that goods or services can be sold and bought.

Comment This answer gives the main definition of a market in its modern sense. If the question was awarded only one or two marks, such an answer would suffice. However, if more marks were awarded, a longer answer would be required. In modern business, 'market' has a number of other meanings. It also refers to the old-fashioned market place, or street market, which still exists. It can also be used to describe the market for a particular kind of goods or service, e.g. 'There's a large market for new forms of training'. In addition, it can be used as a verb, e.g. 'to market jeans' (see Unit 7). It is also sometimes used to refer to stock markets and dealing in shares, e.g. 'The market was quiet yesterday'. If the question attracted a large number of marks, all of these meanings would need to be given and distinguished from each other. Do make sure that you *always* look at the marks awarded before you answer the question. If you do not, you will find yourself writing far too much for just one or two marks, or writing far too little to obtain all of the ten or twelve marks available!

UNIT 2: KINDS OF BUSINESS
1 Sole proprietors (page 7)

Q1 Two of the following: persistence, enthusiasm, ability to work hard, willingness to take risks, organizational skills, tolerance and patience, knowledge of the business.

Comment There are many alternative answers. However, don't give more than two qualities and don't try to explain them, as you will get no more marks.

Q2 It would be appropriate for a sole proprietor to open a cheese shop as it is easy to set up and there are no complicated legal requirements. It would be easy to run the shop alone without employees. The amount of capital required would not be too great, as some of the equipment needed might be hired instead of purchased.

Comment A cheese shop is quite a good choice for a sole proprietor as it is a niche market (see Unit 6), which is idea for small businesses since it is easier for them to compete with bigger shops. The owner would need to have quite a good knowledge of cheese, but this could be fairly easily acquired, perhaps by working in a similar kind of shop first. The main difficulties would be the legal procedures for acquiring shop premises and the purchase and control of stock.

2 Partnerships (page 9)

Q1 A sleeping partner is a member who has invested money in a partnership but takes no active part in its management.

Comment If you had been asked to 'describe' a sleeping partner and the marks awarded were more than one, you should have added that sleeping partners share the profits of the partnership and its losses, as they are equally responsible with all other partners for any debts.

Q2 a One item could be the amount of capital that each partner should invest. This is to ensure that members know what the initial capital of the partnership will be. It also gives each partner a personal stake in the business and therefore a motivation to succeed.

Comment Usually partners invest equal amounts; but some partnerships have senior partners who invest more than junior partners. This would affect the sharing of profits and, possibly, voting arrangements. This clause in the deed of partnership might also deal with sleeping partners.

Q2 b Another item could state how profits – and losses – would be divided between partners. These are usually equally divided, which avoids any disputes about who has worked harder and contributed more to the firm.

Comments If there are senior and junior partners, profits might be divided unequally in accordance with seniority. The deed would also specify when profits would be paid each year and any other form of remuneration partners might receive. To score full marks, you must mention both the feature of the partnership and why it is included. Instead of the subjects in the answer, you could have dealt with the following items:

- Voting arrangements: partners usually have one vote so that no one feels excluded and no partner can feel aggrieved by any decision that is made. If there are senior and junior partners, the voting might be weighted, with senior partners having more than one vote.
- Procedures for taking on new partners. A partnership is a very intimate form of business relationship. It is therefore most important that new partners should fit in with existing members and be liked by them. The deed of partnership would cover this matter, perhaps by making it obligatory for a new partner to be approved by all the existing partners, or by instituting a trial period before the new partner is accepted.
- Dissolving the partnership. The deed will cover the means of dissolving the partnership or allowing one partner to withdraw. This will cover any period of notice that is required for withdrawal; the payment that might be made to a retiring member; and the way in which the business could be sold.

3 Franchising (page 11)

Q1 A franchiser is a firm which allows another person, the franchisee, to use its own product and to trade under its name, for a regular fee.

Comment Note that 'franchiser' is sometimes spelt 'franchisor'.

Q2 A royalty payment is payment that is made for using another person's or firm's product, property or invention. It is a percentage of the sales price, often ten per cent.

Comment You would need to cover all of these points to get full marks. You could have given an example from outside the franchise world. For example, pop stars get a royalty from the record company for every CD they sell. Authors get royalties from their publishers on the sale of their books.

Q3 The main differences between a sole proprietor and a franchisee are:

- A franchisee has less independence than a sole proprietor, but a much bigger chance of success.
- A sole proprietor owns the business and can sell it if he/she wishes. A franchisee usually has to obtain the franchiser's permission.
- A franchisee must continue to make royalty payments.
- A sole proprietor may find it more difficult to borrow from a bank.

Comment The failure rate of franchisees is very low. On average, there are only about seven per cent who fail, with another three per cent giving up the business voluntarily. The initial cost of setting up as a franchisee with a reputable, nationally known franchiser is quite high – in the region of £40,000–£50,000 or more. Smaller firms charge much less, but the risks are much higher.

4 Limited companies (page 13)

Q1 The nominal value of a share is the original price at which it was issued. Its current price, or value, may be much more – or less – than the nominal value.

Comment The price of shares fluctuates more in plcs than they do in private companies, as they are traded day-by-day on the Stock Exchange where they react immediately to any news about the company - rising if it is good news, and falling if it is bad.

Q2 Shares in a plc can be bought and sold by members of the general public, while shares in a private limited company can be sold only to close associates, with the approval of the other shareholders.

The minimum share capital in a plc is £50,000, but in a private limited company, there is no minimum.

Comment Other differences between plcs and private companies include:
- Few shareholders in a plc work in the firm, while a high percentage often do in private companies.
- It is usually easier and quicker to sell shares in a plc than it is in a private company.
- A public limited company has plc after its name, whereas a private limited company has Ltd.
- A public limited company must have at least two shareholders, while, under European Union law, one person can now form a private limited company.

UNIT 3: OBJECTIVES AND ORGANIZATION
1 The need for profit (page 15)

Q1 Turnover is a business's total sales or revenue.

Comment Turnover is expressed in pounds, such as £80,000, and usually relates to a year's trading. Note that 'turnover' is also used in other contexts. Stock turnover means the number of times the stock – or finished goods – is replaced, or turned over, during the year. Labour turnover is the number of employees who leave a business during a year. This is usually expressed as a percentage.

Q2 Profit is the difference between the total revenue produced by sales and all the costs of operating a business. A business's profit usually refers to profit for a whole year. It is essential for all businesses in the private sector to make a profit. If they did not do so, they would not survive, as they would not be able to pay their employees, their shareholders and their bills. In addition, profit can help to increase a business's efficiency by cutting costs and to encourage it to take risks by developing new products. It is also one way of measuring business success.

Comment The word 'explain' in the question shows that a full answer is required. This is borne out by the number of lines allotted to the question, which might be five or six, and the maximum number of marks, which might be six. You should always check both the number of marks and the number of lines allowed for the answer in the question paper before you attempt the question. In this case, a brief answer, such as 'Profit is the difference between sales revenue and total costs', would have obtained only one mark, even though it is totally correct.

Q3 Fifty per cent.

Comment The profit at the beginning of the year was £10,000 (40,000 – 30,000 = 10,000). The profit at the end of the year was £15,000 (45,000 – 30,000 = 15,000). Therefore profit had increased by £5,000 or 50 per cent.

2 Other business objectives (page 17)

Q1 A product-oriented firm will be concerned mainly with making the most durable and high-quality goods, which are superior to their competitor's products. The main emphasis will be on the quality of the product, rather than the customers' wants.

A market-oriented firm will find out first what their customers want (or what they really want without knowing it!). The firm will then make a high-quality product that will satisfy this want. Manufacturers of consumer durables will produce improved and modified versions once the product has been successfully launched, so that people will want to buy the updated version.

Comment Firms in the tertiary sector also provide market-oriented products. For example, banks have many different kinds of accounts for personal customers, business customers, young people, charities, etc., which are all designed to appeal to one particular part – or segment – of the market.

Q2 A firm increases its market share by increasing its sales, or turnover. Although this may involve lowering its prices for a time to gain sales from its rivals, when the firm has gained a larger share of the market, it will be able to raise its prices again. Its profits will increase as its sales and its prices rise. Once it has gained a secure place in the market, banks will be more willing to lend it money because they know that it is a successful firm.

Comment Another benefit for firms that increase their market share is that they will find it much easier to attract better-quality employees, as they know they are more likely to prosper in a successful firm. In business, success breeds more success.

3 Scale and mergers (page 20)

Q1 One example would be a chain of boutiques taking over a clothing manufacturer.

Comment It is useful to remember one example of key terms like this so that you can use it whenever required. Questions of this kind receive only one mark. If you had been asked to describe the benefits as well, it would have been two or three marks. (The main benefits are controlling supplies, so that the manufacturer produces the kind of clothes required, and certainty of supplies, so that they will be delivered on time.)

Q2 Mass production methods produce technical economies of scale through the use of specialized labour and the latest machines. This makes production more efficient, which reduces the cost of making each unit.

Bigger firms get financial economies of scale because the banks will usually let them borrow more money and give them a lower rate of interest.

Comments You were asked to state the benefits of two economies of scale. If you had only described the economies and not explained the benefits, you would have received only half marks at the most. Similarly, if you had given more than two economies of scale and explained their benefits, you would obtain no more than the maximum number of marks.

In this case, you were asked to explain the benefits of economies of scale in general terms only. If the question had been asked in connection with a case study, you would have had to show how that particular firm would have benefited by giving specific examples. For instance, if it had been a wholesaler, the distribution economy would have been using bigger lorries that can carry more goods.

You must remember to read every question thoroughly before you attempt to answer it, and answer only the questions that the examiner has asked.

Instead of one of the economies of scale mentioned above, you could have dealt with buying economies of scale. These produce benefits because suppliers will give a discounts for very large orders.

Another alternative would be risk-bearing economies. Big companies usually operate in several markets and/or countries, which produces risk-bearing economies of scale, as a fall in demand is not likely to happen in all of them at the same time.

Other suitable alternatives would be management, distribution and marketing economies of scale, which make these activities proportionately cheaper because they are spread over a larger number of products.

Q3 a It was a lateral takeover, as the two firms have similar products that do not compete directly with each other.

Comment If Don Bartlett had been a baker without a shop, it would have been a vertical forward merger as he would have been in the secondary sector of production taking over a business in the tertiary sector. However, he is in both sectors of production already as a baker and a retailer, so it was a lateral takeover.

Q3 b The main benefit is risk-bearing economies of scale, as his risks are now spread over two different kinds of market.

Comment There may also be benefits through other economies of scale, such as technical, financial or management.

4 Organizational structures (page 24)

Q1 The main advantage is the division of labour. Each department specializes in one particular task, such as finance, which means that the staff have greater knowledge, skills and experience in that area of business.

Comment There are also management economies of scale, as it is easier to supervise and control people who are all doing similar kinds of work. There is also less chance of any duplication of work.

Q2 A chain of command is the different levels in an organization through which decisions or orders have to pass before they can be put into effect. If there is a long chain of command, it will take some time for an order to reach the person who is going to carry it out, as it may have to go through six or seven levels. It could also become garbled on the way. If the order has come from the top of the organization, the workers who eventually receive it may feel very remote from the person who issued it, whom they may never have even seen or met.

Comment To avoid the disadvantages of having a long chain of command, many organizations have cut out some intermediate levels of authority so that there are now only four or five levels of authority instead of six or seven.

Q3 A span of control is the number of subordinates a manager controls. It will be easier for a manager to delegate more authority to his or her subordinates if both the manager and the subordinates are skilled, experienced and competent. If there were a very rigid system of authority, where many decisions had to be referred to higher levels, the span of control would not be so wide.

Comments This is a good answer as far as it goes. In questions of this kind, it is a good idea to define the key term in the question – 'span of control'. The first example of a wide span of control is valid, but the second is an example of a narrow span of control, which was not what the question asked.

The answer should have explained that a wide span of control is when a manager controls a large number of subordinates. In addition to the example given in the answer, a wide span of control is possible when the work is simple, because few big decisions have to be made. A wide span is also possible when the manager and the subordinates all work in the same place, as their work is then easier to supervise.

5 Problems of multinationals (page 26)

Q1 A big company may have too many levels of management which would make it more difficult to reach decisions and would increase the salary bill.

Employees may lose enthusiasm if they feel the company bosses are distant and inaccessible.

Comments There are a number of alternative answers.

You could have mentioned instead that communications can become more difficult, which means that decisions may not be put into effect and that feedback may be difficult.

Managers may lose any entrepreneurial spirit because the big firm has its own way of doing things which stifles individual actions. As a result, the firm may become uncompetitive.

There may be quarrels between subsidiary companies or between the parent company and its subsidiaries which will weaken the whole organization.

Q2 It is much cheaper for them to set up franchises than it is to open a chain of shops themselves. It also simplifies the control of the foreign business.

Comment Another big advantage is that the franchisees will have greater knowledge of their own domestic market and many useful contacts.

UNIT 4: FINANCE

1 Costs and budgets (page 29)

Q1 One example of a variable cost is raw materials, and one example of a fixed cost is rent.

Comment There are many other examples of variable costs, such as overtime and petrol, and of fixed costs, such as rates and insurance. But don't waste your time by giving more than one example.

Q2 a The total costs were £415.

Comment If you have not got the right answer, add up all the items again.

Q2 b The fixed costs were £195 and the variable costs were £220.

Comment The fixed costs, which do not change from month to month, were: rent £80; business rates £50; interest on bank loan £25; heat, light and power £40 = £195. The variable costs, which change in accordance with how much work is done, were: paint, paper, canvas, etc. £70; models' fees £85; travel £35; post and packing £30 = £220. You can check that your calculations are correct by adding the two totals together, which should be the same as the grand total of £415.

Q2 c The percentage of fixed costs was 47 per cent and the percentage of variable costs was 53 per cent.

Comments The percentage of fixed costs is calculated in the following way:

£195 ÷ £415 × 100 = 46.98%

The percentage of variable costs is calculated in a similar way.

£220 ÷ £415 × 100 = 53.02%

Unless you are asked to do otherwise, percentages should be rounded off to the nearest whole number, so your answers should be 47 per cent for fixed costs and 53 per cent for variable costs. These should add up to 100, which they do.

Q3 It is important for a business to have a budget because it will be able to set definite objectives that it wants to achieve in the following year. It will also set financial targets for the business to achieve. Another benefit is that it enables the business to keep its expenses under control.

If there are any differences between the forecast and the actual results, the reasons for the differences can be investigated and any necessary action can be taken. Sometimes, it may be found that the forecast itself was too optimistic in view of other circumstances, so the firm would need to make sure that more realistic forecasts were produced in the future. If the forecasts are based on reasonable grounds, the budget provides a good measure of the firm's success in exceeding some of its targets.

Comments Many general questions of this kind about major topics in business studies have a high number of maximum marks. Check the maximum mark before you start.

This is a good, comprehensive answer which would obtain the maximum number of marks if it had been slightly better expressed.

One of the great drawbacks of the budgetary system is that managers commonly overestimate their department's needs, so that they will obtain a bigger share of the firm's expenditure; or they may underestimate what they can achieve so that it will be easier for them to reach or exceed their target.

2 Cash and cash flow (page 32)

Q1 Cash is a liquid asset which can be used to pay bills immediately.

Comments This does not answer the question. It gives one example of a liquid asset, but it does not state the difference between liquid and non-liquid assets, or explain 'liquidity' or 'asset'. Assets are everything that a business owns. Liquid assets, such as cash or funds in current or instant-access accounts, can be used immediately to buy goods or services or pay bills; non-liquid assets, such as funds in deposit accounts, cannot be used immediately, and fixed assets, such as land, have to be sold first before they can be used.

Q2 John's costs are so minimal that there is very little chance of his being able to reduce them by very much. All that he might do is to reduce his advertising. Lawn mowing is carried out for only six months or so of the year and hedge-cutting is even more seasonal. Therefore it is unnecessary for John to have advertisements in the local paper every week of the year. In the winter, he could reduce the number of times they appear, or stop them altogether. He might also see if he could reschedule his appointments so that he had shorter journeys and thus save on the running costs of his van.

Comment In this type of question, you will have to use common sense and your own knowledge to find a satisfactory answer. Note that most of the classic ways of cutting costs – such as moving to cheaper premises, delaying maintenance, finding new suppliers – do not apply to John.

Q3 £7,000

Comments Your calculations of the cash flow should be as follows:

£s	June	July	August
Cash inflow	24,500	36,000	23,500
Cash outflow	22,000	30,000	29,000
Net cash flow	2,500	6,000	(5,500)
Opening bank balance	4,000	6,500	12,500
Closing bank balance	6,500	12,500	7,000

The net cash flow is the difference between the cash inflow and cash outflow. This is then added to (or subtracted from) the opening bank balance. Note that negative or minus numbers in accounts are brackets.

3 Breakeven analysis (page 34)

Q1 The variable costs may not be accurate and the revenue curve may not be correct.

Comments This brief answer would score the full two marks – one for each point. Note that if you had been asked to 'explain' or 'describe' the limitations, you would have had to include an explanation also, e.g. 'The variable costs may not be accurate as they may increase as output rises' and 'The revenue curve may not be correct because it is assumed that all goods are sold and that the price of them does not change'. However, if you had given these answers to the current question, you would still have scored no more than two marks – and you would have wasted your own (and the examiner's) time!

Q2 The breakeven point is 3,000 units and the chart would look like this:

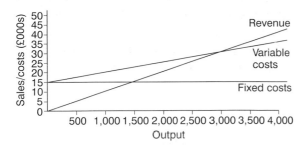

Comment The breakeven point is calculated by the formula:

$$\frac{\text{fixed costs}}{\text{selling price} - \text{variable costs}}$$

In this case, therefore, it would be:

$$\frac{15,000}{10 - 5} = 3,000$$

4 Internal sources of finance (page 37)

Q1 After a plc has paid tax on its profits, it uses them in two main ways. Some is distributed to ordinary and preference shareholders as dividends in return for investing in the company. The rest is retained in the business until it is needed for buying new assets or expansion.

Comment This is a competent answer. The business keeps the retained profit in its reserves. The accumulated amount is shown in the annual balance sheet under the heading 'profit and loss account'.

Q2 The reducing-balance method of depreciation gives a percentage allowance every year. The straight line has the same amount.

Comments This answer would score only a few marks as it does not give a full explanation of the differences between the two methods. It would have been better to start off with a brief explanation of depreciation itself – the decline in the value of an asset.
The reducing-balance method allows for this fall in value by writing off the same percentage of the asset's value each year. The straight-line method calculates what the allowance would be for each year of the asset's useful life.
The reducing-balance method provides a big allowance in the first years which rapidly reduces, whereas the straight-line method provides the same allowance every year.

5 External sources of finance (page 42)

Q1 Thirty days.

Comment Under a new law, firms which exceed the stated period of credit can now be sued for the money, plus interest.

Q2 There are differences in repayments and ownership. With hire purchase, a deposit usually has to be paid and repayments are usually made monthly. With leasing, there is usually no deposit and repayments are made at regular intervals, not necessarily monthly.

With hire purchase, the goods are owned when the last instalment has been paid; with leasing, the goods are never owned.

Comment With assets such as vehicles, the lessee (the business or person who has taken out the lease) receives a proportion of the amount for which the asset is sold at the end of the lease. With property, however, the building reverts to the freeholder at the end of the lease, and the lessee receives nothing.

Q3 a £43,500

Comment £14,500 × 3 = £43,500

Q3 b £53,940

Comment £43,500 ÷ 100 × 12 = £5,220 × 2 = £10,440 + £43,500 = £53,940

Q3 c It would be better to pay cash, as Mustapha would not have to pay interest.

Comments This answer is substantially correct, but it is a little bare, and would only be a Level 2 answer at best. The candidate could have added further details to gain a higher mark. It is obvious that Mustapha's firm is cash rich, as he has nearly a quarter of a million pounds in his deposit account. Moreover, the firm is making very handsome profits, so more money will be streaming in. It is only useful to buy on hire purchase when you are short of cash. So Mustapha should pay for the cars outright, or, even better, find some more profitable use for his money on deposit.

Unit 5: Accounts
1 Business accounts (page 45)

Q1 a management accountants

b balance sheet

c auditors

d consistency

Comment You will sometimes find questions like this at the beginning of the exam paper, just to give you an easy start for four marks.

Q2 Trade unions read final accounts to see if companies are profitable enough to give high wage rises. Banks also read them to see if their loans are in secure hands.

Comments It is a waste of time to give reasons when you are not asked to do so, as this candidate has done, because you will gain no more marks. Alternative answers are: suppliers, creditors, companies in the same kind of business and companies looking for other companies to take over.

Q3 Firms keep accounts to have a complete record of all their present and past financial transactions, to forecast what is likely to happen in the future and to compare their results with those of similar firms.

Comment A good answer as far as it goes, but the legal obligation for all businesses to keep accounts must also be included.

2 Trading accounts (page 49)

Q1 So that they know how much money they have made.

Comments This is a useless answer which will score no marks. The candidate should have first defined gross profit, which is the difference between the cost of goods sold and turnover or sales. The gross profit margin is a ratio which is calculated by expressing the gross profit as a percentage of sales. This ratio can be used to compare the business's performance with those of previous years and with the gross profit margins of firms in the same kind of business. If there was a high maximum mark for this question, you should also give an actual example; or if the question relates to a case study, you should refer back to that for your example.

Q2a Cost of sales was £110,000 and gross profit was £90,000.

Comments A correct answer, but to gain full marks, you would also need to put in the final debit and credit lines, which are also missing from the account. These were:
200,000   200,000
The complete trading account would look like this:

Sales		200,000
Opening stock	80,000	
Purchases	120,000	
less closing stock	90,000	
Cost of sales		110,000
Gross profit		90,000
	200,000	200,000

Q2b The gross profit margin was 45 per cent.

Comment The workings are:
$$\frac{90,000}{200,000} \times 100 = 45\%$$

Q3a 4.5 times

Comment The workings are £365,000 ÷ £81,000 = 4.5

Q3b 3 times

Comment This calculation has to be done in two parts. First, find the average stock by adding the opening and closing stock and dividing by two.
(£42,000 + £58,000) ÷ 2 = £50,000
Then find the stock turnover rate by dividing the cost of sales by average stock:
£150,000 ÷ £50,000 = 3 times

3 Profit and loss accounts (page 51)

Q1 Operating profit is the actual profit that remains after the cost of sales and all the overheads have been taken away from the sales or turnover.

Comment You should remember that 'operating profit' is the same as 'net profit'.

Q2 Rent, business rates and insurance.

Comment There is a large choice here. You could have mentioned interest charges, electricity and gas, wages and salaries, advertising, depreciation, etc.

Q3a £838

Comment The correct answer is £838,000. It's quite a common mistake to forget to add 000 to 838, so be careful in future if you have made this mistake here. ('Net profit' is the same as 'operating profit'.)

Q3b Eighteen per cent.

Comments Note that you were asked to find the gross profit margin, not net profit as in the previous part of the question. You must be very careful, particularly with financial questions, to make sure that you are answering the exact question that has been asked. Do not assume anything. Check the question again before you answer it. The workings were:
£2,800,000 ÷ £15,360,000 × 100 = 18.2%

Q3c It could be compared with the gross profit margin in previous years and the margins of companies in the same kind of business.

Comments The gross profit margin would only indicate how successful a business was in controlling the cost of making goods or the cost of buying and reselling them. The net profit ratio gives a better idea of the total performance of a firm after all expenses have been taken into account. For example, a manufacturer might be very efficient at making goods, but very inefficient in managing the business, so that its overheads were far too high. This would result in a low net profit margin.

4 Balance sheets (page 55)

Q1 Stock and cash at bank are assets; a bank loan, creditors and capital are liabilities.

Comments It may be difficult to think of capital as a liability, but it is easier to understand why if you think of it from the point of view of the business. Capital is the money that the shareholders, the owners, have put into the business. Therefore it is a liability for the business.

It is exactly the same with a sole proprietor. The money that he/she puts into the business to start it up is the capital. This amount of money is owed to him/her and is therefore a liability. If the business were sold, he/she would receive the money and the business's liability would end.

Q2 Fixed assets are items owned by a business which it will keep for a long time. Two examples are land and investments.

Comments Although examples have been given of the two different kinds of assets, the candidate has failed to explain the difference between them in the definition, and would, therefore, not gain full marks. You need to state that there are two kinds of fixed assets: tangible, such as land, buildings, furniture and fittings, vehicles, machinery and equipment; and non-tangible, such as investments. 'Tangible' literally means 'something that can be touched'.

Q3 a The balance sheet.

Comment It is important to know where to find different items in the three final accounts. For example, some students waste time looking for stock in the profit and loss account, when it is actually in the balance sheet and the trading account.

Q3 b The working capital is calculated by subtracting current liabilities from current assets.

Comment 'Working capital' is also known as 'net current assets', or 'net current liabilities' if it is a negative number.

Q3 c It is important because it shows the cash that the business has available to pay its immediate bills and other obligations.

Comment A positive working capital is also needed to pay for the day-to-day running of the company, and for buying stock. Good cash-flow forecasting enables companies to avoid a negative working capital, which causes a cash-flow problem.

5 Balance sheet ratios (page 58)

Q1 2000   1.15:1

   1999   1.12:1

Comment The workings are:
    2000 $120 \div 104 = 1.15$
    1999 $110 \div 98 = 1.12$

Q2 a Company X has a higher net profit margin and is therefore more profitable.

Comments The workings would have to be shown here and in Question 2b to gain full marks. The profitability of businesses can be compared by using the net profit margin ratio.
The net profit margin for Company X is:
       $£2,500,000 \div £12,000,000 \times 100 = 20.8\%$
The net profit margin for Company Y is:
       $£8,000,000 \div £4,500,000 \times 100 = 17.8\%$

Q2 b Company Y is performing more efficiently, as it has a higher ROCE.

Comments The return on capital employed measure how efficiently a business is performing.
The ROCE of Company X is:
       $£2,500,000 \div £20,000,000 \times 100 = 12.5\%$
The ROCE of Company Y is:
       $£800,000 \div £4,000,000 \times 100 = 20\%$
Therefore, Company Y is using its capital more efficiently.

UNIT 6: FINDING A MARKET
1 Different markets (page 62)

Q1 Commodity, organizational, financial and consumer markets.

> **Comment** You could have used the term 'industrial market' instead of 'organizational market'. 'Organizational market' is better, as it covers all kinds of businesses, whereas 'industrial market' refers mainly to manufacturers. If you had been asked to name five kinds of market, you would have included 'traditional markets'.

Q2 Market segmentation helps businesses to increase their market share because they will know which goods or services will appeal most to customers in that segment. It will also help them to design new products that will satisfy the wants of consumers in their segments.

> **Comment** 'Increasing profit through bigger sales' is also an advantage. However, it is a little different from the two advantages given in the answer, as it is a general advantage, while the others are specific advantages.

Q3 A niche market is a special section of a market which is often very small. One example is the niche market for cruises in the foreign holiday market.

> **Comment** This answer is fine. There are many other kinds of niche markets – ties in the male clothes market, hockey equipment in the sports market, etc.

2 Market research (page 65)

Q1 a Desk and field market research.

> **Comment** Primary (field) and secondary (desk) research are also acceptable answers.

Q1 b Interviewing consumers is one method of field research; reading government reports is a method of desk research.

> **Comment** There is a wide choice of examples. Some are: (desk) EU reports, local council reports, census returns; (field) hall tests, focus groups, observation, etc.

Q2 a desk research

b field research

c field research

d desk research

> **Comments** These answers are acceptable because the question said 'State'. You will get one mark for each correct answer, making four marks in all. If it had said 'Explain', however, there would probably have been two marks on offer for each, making eight marks in all, and you would have had to give more specific answers. The answers might then have been:
> **a** desk research, using government or motor-industry statistics
> **b** field research, using a consumer survey
> **c** field research, using a consumer survey or, possibly, a focus group if it was desirable to know their deeper reasons and motivations for choosing the newspaper
> **d** desk research, using government statistics or trade statistics from the Audit Bureau of Circulation, which provides more up-to-date figures of newspaper circulation

Q3 The manufacturer could carry out some street interviews to see if people liked the idea.

Comments This is a very poor answer that would score only one of the six or eight marks that might be available. Although it is true that a consumer survey would be carried out, it would probably not be done by the manufacturing company itself, but by a firm specializing in market research. The candidate should have stated that desk research should first be used to discover whether the market for chocolate bars was sufficiently buoyant for a new product to be introduced. Statistics about sales in the past and the present, and forecasts for future sales, could be obtained from official and unofficial reports and from the manufacturer's own files.
Field research would then have been used to study consumer reaction to the new bar. This could be carried out by means of a consumer survey and by a hall test of the bar itself.

UNIT 7: MARKETING
I Product (page 67)

QI Product, price, promotion, place.

Comment No further information is required to gain four marks.

Q2 The chain would increase its profits by selling own-brand goods, as it would no longer have to pay such a high price to the suppliers of branded goods. It could shop around among suppliers who could make similar goods to the brand to obtain the best possible price for its supplies. The size of the order would ensure that it was in a strong bargaining position. It could then sell its own brand at a lower price than the original and still make a bigger profit. If its own-brand products provided popular, the number of visitors to the shops – and sales – would rise.

Comment This is a very good answer. The candidate could have stated that another advantage would be the goodwill that own-brand products create. This would increase the market value of the business if it was sold.

2 Product life cycles (page 69)

QI Introduction, growth, maturity, saturation, decline.

Comment These terms are normally used to describe the five stages. You may sometimes see the three first stages called launch, early growth and late growth instead, but it is advisable to stick to the usual terms.

Q2 A product range describes the similar kinds of goods that a firm makes, such as knives of all kinds – from cook's knives to table knives and throwing knives.

A product mix describes all the different kinds of goods that a firm makes, such as knives, razors, swords, etc.

Comments These two terms apply not only to manufacturers but to service providers. A bank therefore might have a range of current accounts for different kinds of customers, such as personal, business and charities; and a mix of financial services, including investment, insurance, mortgage, trust management, etc. Note that you were asked to 'describe', so you must give examples to gain full marks.

Q3 The firm might try to find a new use for them by selling them singly as computer mouse mats. Alternatively, they might try producing personalized versions of their table mats for cafés and restaurants.

Comments These are excellent suggestions, as it is unlikely that improved versions of the product or new packaging would increase sales. A price reduction would reduce profits even further and probably produce no great increase in sales, as the market for these products is in decline because of the reasons stated in the question.

3 Price (page 71)

Q1 At the entrance to a supermarket.

Comment It might also be found in any store.

Q2 a critical price point

b discounts

Comment 'Loyalty card points' would also be a valid answer;

Q2 c penetration price

Comment 'Skimming price' is an alternative answer.

Q2 d differential prices

Q3 Cost-plus pricing is when a manufacturer calculates the cost of making the product and then adds on the overheads and the profit required to find the selling price. For example, a product might cost £1 to make. The overhead costs, per unit, are 30p. The manufacturer wants a mark-up of 20 per cent, which would be 20p. The selling price would therefore be £1.50.

Comments The definition in the first part of the answer is fine. The candidate could have used the term 'variable costs' instead of 'the cost of making the product' and 'fixed costs' instead of 'overheads'. However, the calculations in the example are wrong, so he/she would not have scored full marks. He/She has allowed for mark-up only on the variable costs and not the total costs. The correct calculations are:

Unit cost + overheads = £1.30

Mark-up required = 20 per cent.

Therefore, mark-up would be:

£1.30 × 20 ÷ 100 = £0.26.

Therefore the selling price would be

£1.30 + £0.26 = £1.56.

4 Promotion (page 76)

Q1 They provide a great range of advertisements, from small classified ads to big display advertisements at varying costs. It is easy to choose a newspaper that will cover the target market segment. Advertisements can be cut out of the paper and kept for future reference. They often contain reply coupons for further information or purchasing the goods advertised.

Comment This is an excellent answer, as the candidate has covered all the main points. Note that newspapers provide advertisers with a full breakdown of their readership by socio-economic group and gender, which makes it much easier to target market segments.

Q2 a They could advertise their restaurant in the local newspaper. If they had very little capital, they could use classified advertisements, but it would be better to use a display advertisement first, as that would have more impact.

Comments They could also distribute handbills to local houses. This provides blanket coverage and is also very cheap. Before they opened, they could also have a large poster in the shop window or on the wall above the restaurant (subject to any necessary planning permission). However, this could be quite expensive, as the poster would need to be professionally designed and printed if it was not to harm the business's image.

Q2 b The main advantage of advertising in the local newspaper is that they would be likely to reach their target segments, as most of their customers are likely to be local. It would also tell people where the restaurant was situated and the date it was opening.

Comments The newspaper advertisement would also make potential customers aware of the kinds of meals that would be served and their prices. The chosen meals – fish and chips or pan-fried scallops with dill and lime – would help create an image of the business.

Q2c David and Sue could have special offers for the opening night. For example, they could give a free bottle of house wine to every couple.

> **Comment** They might also give customers discount vouchers that gave ten per cent off their next meal.

Q3a Discount vouchers.

> **Comment** There are many alternatives, such as free gifts, competitions, bonus packs, etc.

Q3b Discount vouchers on bars of chocolate and on jars of coffee, which give the customer a reduction on the next purchase.

> **Comment** Discounts are not necessarily given only on next purchase. Some give a discount for the first purchase.

Q3c The main problem is that sales promotions often produce only a short-term boost in sales, unless they are available for a long period of time.

> **Comments** There is also a danger that popular promotions may be greatly over-subscribed. The classic example was the free flight offer made to buyers of Hoover products in the early 1990s. There were so many takers that it took the company many months and a large amount of money to satisfy all the customers who wanted a free flight.

5 Place and packaging (page 79)

Q1 Selling the goods to a wholesaler means that the manufacturer does not have to deliver them to hundreds of shops and stores. The wholesaler also breaks bulk by repackaging the goods into smaller quantities, which allows the manufacturer to concentrate on making the goods instead of sorting them into small lots.

> **Comment** The wholesaler also provides storage space for the manufacturer's goods.

Q2 The main kind of direct marketing a hotel could use is sending letters to its previous customers at regular intervals with either a discount voucher or a special offer. This is a very cheap method, as the names should already be stored on a database, and it should have a quite high response rate, as the customers have stayed at the hotel before.

Another method would be advertisements, with reply-paid coupons, in newspapers or magazines. The publications would have to be carefully selected to make sure that the readership matched the market segments that might use the hotel. The hotel's own database would give some indications of what the segments are.

This method is much more expensive than direct mail, but it has one big advantage. It would attract new customers, which is essential if a business is to expand and survive.

The Internet would provide a third means of direct marketing. This is comparatively cheap, and has the big advantage of giving global coverage.

> **Comments** This is an excellent answer, which covers all the main points. Some hotels also send out Christmas cards to previous customers. These may help to boost the hotel's image, but they are unlikely to produce many bookings, unless the cards are linked with special offers, which some customers might resent.

UNIT 8: RETAILING AND BANKING
1 Retailing (page 82)

Q1 Meat and vegetables; their own bank and dry-cleaning services.

> **Comment** There is a wide choice of answer for goods, e.g. designer clothes, perfume, newspapers, plants and kitchen equipment, and for services, e.g. pharmacy, photo processing and cafeteria. Everyone should get four marks!

Q2 The main advantage is that less stock has to be kept on the premises, as electronic ordering systems make it possible to deliver goods just-in-time. This saves interest charges, as less money has to be borrowed to buy stock, and rents are reduced as less storage space is needed.

Comments The candidate has stated some advantages, but missed the main ones. The chief benefit is cutting out the wholesaler's profit, which enables retailers to reduce prices or to increase their own profit margins. This also gives them greater control over distribution and suppliers. These benefits are only available to multiple retailers. Small corner shops can join voluntary buying groups, which purchase goods in bulk and sell them to members at low prices.

2 Banks and finance houses (page 85)

Q1 A bank is a public limited company. A building society is a mutual society that is owned by its members.

Comments This is the main difference. There are also other differences. A bank deals in a wider range of services; often has branches overseas; and usually has much greater net assets than a building society.

Q2 Wholesale funds are cheaper because there are fewer administrative, or over-the-counter, costs.

Comments The answer is correct, but it is incomplete and would therefore get few marks. With questions of this type, which are very common, you must first define the terms. Wholesale funds are obtained on money markets where big organizations borrow money they require and lend their spare cash. Retail funds are deposited by customers in a bank or building society branch. Because retail deposits are often for very small amounts, the cost of administration, even using computers, is relatively high.
In contrast, just one transaction on the money markets might raise millions of pounds. Money markets charge lower rates of interest on the money borrowed because they have smaller administrative costs and because they are lending to other financial institutions.

Q3 During the recession in the early 1990s, when economic activity slowed down, many small businesses were in serious financial trouble. The number of company insolvencies more than doubled between 1988 and 1993. Yet many small businesses found that the banks were unwilling to support them in this period of crisis, and instead raised charges for their loans and called in small business overdrafts.

Small businesses are also offended by the charges that banks make for every small business service, such a providing coins for shopkeepers' small change.

Comments This is an excellent answer which shows that the candidate has acquired a great amount of knowledge about business affairs and also has the ability to use this knowledge intelligently. Some of the other factors might be the reluctance of banks to finance entrepreneurial or risky ventures; mistakes in accounts and delays in counter service.

UNIT 9: PRODUCTION
1 Products and methods (page 89)

Q1 Job production for making a bridge; and batch production for making furniture.

> **Comment** The other method is flow production, which is used for making a great variety of consumer goods, from cars to cameras, and also for industrial goods, such as oil and plastics.

Q2 There would be a great saving in labour costs, as only semi-skilled workers, who are paid lower wages than skilled workers, are needed on the assembly line. The output would also increase.

> **Comments** This is a very good answer as far as it goes, but it does not go quite far enough, so it would not obtain full marks. The output would increase because there is now a continuous production process, which eliminates the need for moving semi-finished goods from one section of the plant to another. As workers are doing only one simple job all the time, their productivity, or rate of work, rises so that the speed at which the assembly line moves can be gradually increased to a maximum rate. This rise in productivity reduces unit costs.

Q3 When Adrian worked on the assembly line, he did the same job time after time all day long. The work was very boring and monotonous, but also quite hard, as he had to keep up with the moving assembly line, and there was little opportunity for pausing in his work. It was also very noisy and there was little chance of talking to other workers.

It was quite different in his new job. He was in charge of installing his own section of the intricate electrical system in the helicopter. It was very interesting and quite difficult work, so that he always felt a sense of achievement when each helicopter was finished.

> **Comment** This is a very good answer. Adrian would also have found another benefit: his pay could have been two or three times as much!

2 New mass-production methods (page 92)

Q1 Just-in-time is a system of delivering supplies to manufacturers just before they are required. It cuts costs, as interest no longer has to be paid on holding large stocks of parts and raw materials.

> **Comment** It also needs much less storage space in the factory. The firm could move to smaller premises or use the freed space for some other purpose, such as research and development.

Q2 High capital costs and the need to hold large stocks of components.

> **Comment** Other disadvantages are inflexibility, which makes it difficult to produce different versions of a product, and assembly-line workers' boredom and lack of motivation.

Q3 Total quality management would improve the company's products by making them as excellent as possible. The products would be more reliable; there would be fewer defects; and a constant improvement in quality.

This would be achieved by setting up quality circles for shopfloor workers. These small groups would suggest improvements in their way of working and in the product itself.

Because it is a total system, there would also be quality circles in all the other departments of the company. These would be concerned with improvement in their work and in the reputation of the company. Managers would need to be constantly searching for ways in which the company's internal and external quality could be improved. This would probably involve much more training and retraining of staff; and more concern with ethical, or moral, aspects of company policy, such as the impact of its products on the environment, and its relationship with the local community and with the developing world.

> **Comment** This is an excellent answer, covering both aspects of TQM very well.

Unit 10: People in Business

1 Job motivation (page 95)

Q1 Job rotation would make workers feel less bored, as they would be getting a change by doing different kinds of jobs from time to time. Job enlargement would have similar effects, as they would do slightly different jobs instead of the same job all the time. Job enrichment would increase their sense of responsibility and their job satisfaction because they would be in charge of a whole project.

Comment This is a very good answer. Team work involves all three methods of job improvement by giving a group of workers complete control of a job and full responsibility for it as well as opportunities to do any job of which they are capable.

Q2 Structural unemployment is caused when old industries, such as coal mining, are replaced by new industries, such as natural gas and nuclear power.

Cyclical unemployment results from periodic slumps in the economy, which are then followed by booms, when employment picks up again.

Comments You should also say how long the effect of the unemployment might last, i.e. structural unemployment is likely to be permanent, whereas cyclical unemployment usually lasts for a shorter time.
Two other forms of unemployment are:
Technological unemployment, which involves a permanent loss of jobs as workers are replaced by machines.
Frictional unemployment, when workers transfer from one sector of production to another, which is usually temporary. For example, a coal miner might lose his job in the primary sector. He would be unemployed while he tried to find a new job in a factory (secondary sector) or supermarket (tertiary sector).

Q3 Permanent full-time jobs are replaced by temporary jobs, part-time work or short-term contracts.

Comments This answer is inadequate, as it only explains what flexible working is and doesn't deal with its effects on the company, which was what the examiner asked.
There would be numerous effects on the company. The main benefit would be the saving in costs and in the need to provide other social benefits of employment, such as pensions and redundancy payments. Some of these workers are also paid at a lower relative rate than full-time workers, which would also save costs. There would also be some disadvantages. Part-time and temporary workers tend to have less loyalty to the company, so they might not be as highly motivated as full-time employees. The company would also lose the knowledge and experience that permanent full-time employees possess. A flexible workforce would also increase permanent staff's workload, as they would have to train temporary staff and correct their mistakes. It could also create a general feeling of insecurity in the firm.

2 Pay and benefits (page 101)

Q1 The immediate effect would be protests from the unions involved, as they would no longer have such a strong position and so much influence in the factories. Many of the workers would also feel hurt, unless the firm was going to introduce higher pay rates or a better pay system. There might be some industrial action, or even a strike.

The protest could go on for months. Some workers might leave their jobs. The best workers might gain, as they might be paid more than their fellow workers, and more than they were paid before. The majority, however, might feel much more insecure, as they would no longer have a union to speak for them.

The company would benefit greatly. Employees would no longer get an automatic pay rise every year. Their pay would depend far more on how hard they worked and their value to the company. There would probably be a great saving in labour costs.

The shareholders would also be pleased as profits would probably rise and they would receive bigger dividends.

Comment To gain full marks, you must mention the effects on trade unions, employees, the company and shareholders.

Q2 Bonuses are usually paid in a lump sum once a year, and vary from year to year, as they are based on an individual's or a firm's performance.

Commissions are usually paid with the salary once a month, and are fixed, as they are based on a percentage of sales.

Comment Bonuses may not be paid at all in some years if profits are low, whereas commission has to be paid, regardless of the firm's profits.

Q3 The gross pay, which is composed of the basic wage or salary plus all additional payments, is worked out first. Compulsory deductions for income tax and National Insurance contributions, and voluntary deductions for a pension, are then made. The amount that remains is the net pay.

Comment Voluntary deductions can also include such items as subscription to trade unions and company clubs, and payment to voluntary savings schemes.

3 The role of trade unions (page 104)

Q1 One effect might be a loss of production.

Comment You do not have to define 'demarcation dispute' as you were only asked to state one effect. Only one mark would be awarded for this type of question. Other effects might be an increase in inter-union friction; loss of management time in trying to solve the dispute; and increase in trade-union power in the workplace.

Q2 A work to rule is when union members observe all the official rules governing their work. This will slow down production throughout the working day and cause a loss of profit, as fewer goods will be produced.

An overtime ban occurs when workers refuse to work longer than the standard hours stated in their contract of employment. This will reduce the amount of goods produced, as many firms rely heavily on overtime to fulfil their production schedules.

Comment Another important difference is that with a work to rule, workers lose no pay; but with an overtime ban, workers will also lose heavily, as about half of all manual workers rely on overtime payments.

Q3 Workers would have to conduct their own negotiations with the owner of the business, or the managers, over pay and other matters, or just accept the terms offered. They would be in a much weaker position, as it is most unlikely that all workers would be willing to act together or agree on what they wanted. They would almost certainly have to accept lower pay, and, possibly, short-term contracts. Their working conditions might also become worse.

Comment Workers would still be able to belong to a union and obtain its advice. But without a union presence in the factory, it would be difficult to put its advice into effect.

UNIT 11: RECRUITMENT AND TRAINING
1 Recruitment (page 109)

Q1 A job description describes the job itself, the duties involved and the responsibilities. A job specification describes the education, skills, experience and the personal qualities that are needed to do the job.

A job description is often shown to the applicant, whereas a job specification rarely is.

Comment A job specification is sometimes called a person specification, which is what it really is!

Q2 It would be best to advertise in a national newspaper, like the Daily Telegraph or the Sunday Times, as they are read by many managers. Alternatively, an executive employment agency would 'head hunt' a suitable manager from another firm, or present a shortlist of available managers to choose from.

Comment You could also advertise in a professional magazine, if a particular skill, such as accountancy, was involved; or you might ask friends in the business world if they knew of any suitable person.

Q3 It is much cheaper and quicker than recruiting external candidates.

Comments Alternative answers are that the skills and character of the candidates are already known; and that they already have a good knowledge of the firm, so they will require little, if any, induction. There is no point in giving more than two advantages, as you will get no more marks.

2 Legal procedures and induction (page 112)

Q1 An employee could be dismissed on the spot if he or she was guilty of fraud or theft.

Comment The firm would have to be absolutely certain of its case, otherwise it could face a legal action that could result in very heavy damages.

Q2 If there was no induction process, new employees would know nothing about the history and aims of the company, or the firm's rules and principles, and its conditions of employment. They would not know where to go for help if they had any problems, or how to find their way round the building physically. They would not know what their job involved, or who their colleagues were.

Comment This answer provides an excellent summary of the results of not having an induction process, but it does not describe the effect on employees. The employees might feel lost, uneasy, insecure and possibly unhappy and neglected. These effects – or something similar – must be included in the answer to score full marks.

3 Training (page 114)

Q1 a The proportion of workers who leave a firm during a year expressed as a percentage.

Comment Labour turnover should not be confused with similar words or phrases. Turnover by itself means annual sales. Stock turnover is the number of times a business turns over its stock during the year.

Q1 b Seven per cent.

Comment The workings are:
$361 \div 5,000 \times 100 = 7.22$

Q2 a Reduced labour turnover.

Comment There are a number of alternatives: higher production, better-quality products, reduction in returned goods and complaints.

Q2 b Higher morale.

Comment Again, there are alternative answers, such as greater skills and more flexibility.

Unit 12: Communication
1 Good communication (page 116)

Q1 It allows receivers to respond to the message by putting their own views.

Comment It also allows the sender to check that the message has been correctly understood.

Q2 The message may have been unclear or too complicated.

Comment There are many other reasons for communication failures. The receiver might have failed to understand the message, or an unsuitable means of communication might have been chosen – a spoken order instead of a full, written command.

2 Methods of communication (page 121)

Q1 A report should have a title, a brief introduction, headings or subheadings for each section, a conclusion, a list of recommendations and the name of the author and the date, usually at the end.

Comment If you are asked to write a report as part of your examination and are not given a format to use, you should use this one.

Q2a A business form would be used only if some simple information had to be given on a routine or standard matter. Any reply would have to be brief, as there is not much space on a form.

Q2b A business letter is far more flexible. A short letter can be used to make a formal acknowledgement; or a much longer letter can be written to explain a complicated matter.

Comment You were asked to 'explain', so examples should be given. Another major difference between a form and a letter is that the letter allows the sender to express his or her views and feelings.

Q3a A fax.

Comment Or an e-mail, if the document was in digital format.

Q3b Talk to them one to one.

Comment Or use the phone or send a letter.

Q3c Arrange a video conference.

Comment This would be much quicker than going to see them, and probably, just as effective.

Q3d Write a report.

Comment There is no real alternative.

Q3e Put up a notice.

Comment If they ignored the notice, you would have to use some other means, such as memos to all heads of department.

Q3f Try the Internet.

Comment The information you want may well be on some site; the only trouble – very often – is finding it.

Q3g Give a presentation.

Comment A video conference might be used if they were not all in the same place.

Unit 13: Information Technology
1 IT in manufacturing (page 123)

Q1 The difference is that CAD (computer-assisted design) uses computers to design goods, and CAM (computer-assisted manufacturing) uses computer-controlled machines to make the goods.

Comment If a manufacturing firm uses CAD, it almost invariably also uses CAM. The system is then referred to as CAD/CAM.

Q2 Robots can work 24 hours a day and can be used in dangerous or unhealthy environments.

Comment They are also cheaper and more accurate than human labour and need less human management.

2 Distribution and IT (page 126)

Q1 Automatic communication between computers.

Comment Electronic data exchange (EDI) is used in supermarkets to order more goods automatically from regional distribution centres when stock is running low.

Q2 An EPOS system is an electronic point-of-sale system which automatically records sales on a computer when a bar code on a label or a tag is passed under a laser beam.

This system has many advantages for the retailer. It enables the firm to keep a constant check on the stock level in each branch and to deliver any replacements required just-in-time before the stock runs out. This reduces costs, as less storage space is needed at each branch; interest payments are lower, as only a minimal amount of stock has to be kept; and fewer office workers have to be employed, as ordering is done automatically.

EPOS is usually linked with a highly automated warehouse system, using the latest computer-controlled shelf stackers, which also cuts labour costs. The headquarters of the firm can also keep a constant check on how goods are selling in each branch. This makes it much easier for headquarters to increase, reduce, or phase in orders from their suppliers for particular garments in accordance with sales throughout the group.

Comment This is an excellent answer which would get full marks.

Unit 14: Government Influence

1 Government policy (page 129)

Q1 a The Bank of England

Comment Changes in interest rates are decided by the Bank's monetary policy committee. In the last resort, the Chancellor of the Exchequer still retains final control over interest rates. However, the Chancellor would only intervene if there was a serious financial crisis.

Q1 b Inflation is an ongoing rise in the general level of prices.

Comment British inflation has been reduced in the last few years, so it is now one of the lowest in the EU.

Q1 c A rise in interest rates helps to cut inflation as it reduces demand.

Comment It will also tend to stop businesses and individuals from borrowing money. This reduces the amount of money in circulation, which will also tend to reduce investment and demand in the economy.

Q2 £1,200

Comment The workings are:
$$10.5\% - 9.7\% = 0.8\%$$
$$£150,000 \times \tfrac{0.8}{100} = £1,200$$

2 Government restraints (page 131)

Q1 a Under British law, a monopoly situation might arise if a business controls 25 per cent or more of one market.

Comment It could also arise if a merger involved taking over assets worth £70 million or more.

Q1 b The Director General of the Office of Fair Trading.

Comment Occasionally, the Trade Secretary will ask the Competition Commission to investigate a merger directly.

Q1 c If the Director General thinks that the merger would be against the public interest, he or she can recommend to the Trade Secretary that it should be investigated by the Competition Commission.

Comment The Director General can also recommend to the Trade Secretary that no action should be taken if the merger does not appear to be against the public interest.

Q2 It forces businesses such as banks, that offer credit to the public, to state the true cost of borrowing the money, or the APR, the annual percentage rate of interest. The Act also prevents businesses from inviting people under 18 years of age to buy goods on credit or to borrow money.

Comment The Act also: gives a cooling-off period of several days for credit agreements that were signed at home; introduced licences for businesses giving credit; and restricted mortgage brokers' charges for offers that were not taken up.

3 Government aid to business (page 133)

Q1 a An enterprise zone is an area in an inner city which has a high rate of unemployment.

Comment It is usually a relatively small area with other signs of social deprivation, such as poor housing, lack of play areas, closed shops, etc.

Q1 b One benefit would be paying a lower level of business rates, or none at all.

Comment Other benefits are easier planning permission, capital allowances, possibly grants.

Q2 a Development areas.

Comment The aid is only given if jobs are created.

Q2 b The area around Glasgow.

Comment Other areas are parts of Liverpool, Manchester and Newcastle upon Tyne, and the south-western regions of Wales and Cornwall.

UNIT 15: SOCIAL RESPONSIBILITIES
1 Choosing a business location (page 138)

Q1 One important factor is choosing a suitable site. For example, a manufacturer of large machines would need a site with easy access for large lorries and sufficient turning areas.

External economies of scale are also important for some businesses. A solicitor might open a business near other solicitors as they might pass on cases to him/her if they had too much work already.

A pleasant local environment is another important factor. This may make it easier to recruit staff.

Comments Other possible factors, and examples, are:
- Grants: given by the government in assisted areas if jobs are created and by the European Union to firms in deprived areas.
- Nearness to market and/or suppliers: shops need to be in crowded streets or in out-of-town developments.
- Transport links: nearness to motorways is important for manufacturers for obtaining supplies and for despatching goods.
- Suitable workforce: some areas of the country, such as the West Midlands, have many skilled car workers because of their long engineering tradition.

There are many other valid examples.

Q2 a The factors mentioned for both shops are suitability of sites and premises; nearness to market; and the local environment.

Comment This answer is correct.

Q2 b If permission for change of use was needed, the local authority would have to be asked.

Comment Another factor that might be important is a suitable workforce, and especially, the level of wages. The possibility of obtaining a grant might be another factor. As a sole proprietor, Karen might qualify for some form of government grant for starting up a new business. This would depend on her personal circumstances.

Q2c Although the rent and rates of Shop A are relatively cheap, a large amount of money would have to be spent on refitting. It is in a drab area, with total parking restrictions, half a mile away from a high street, so it is unlikely to attract many customers.

Shop B is more expensive to rent, but little money has to be spent on it immediately, which is an important factor when a business is started. It is situated in a smart area, which would be particularly useful if Karen is thinking of selling up-market clothes.

Shop B seems to be the clear winner. Before she decides, Karen should carry out an observation survey to see how many people and of what type visit the street during the day.

Comment This is a very good answer. In questions of this kind, you must give the reasons for your choice. Stating only Shop A or Shop B would gain few marks – or none at all.

2 Social costs and benefits (page 141)

Q1 The term means both the private costs of an action to the business concerned and the external costs of that action to the rest of society. For example, if a club opened in a residential street, one of the costs for the club owner would be the purchase of the premises, and one of the external costs would be the increase in noise for local residents.

Comment The phrase 'and give one example of each' clearly shows that you are expected to treat social costs as covering both private and external costs.

Q2 Some of the social costs might be: greater noise and other forms of pollution; increased traffic congestion; greater danger of accidents; reduced house values; loss of countryside.

Some of the social benefits might be: more jobs at the airport; greater opportunities to open businesses; new firms attracted to the area.

Comment The phrase 'for the locality' shows that only the effects on the neighbourhood are wanted, not the private, or the national, costs and benefits.

Q3 A pressure group is a band of people who try to persuade an organization in the public or private sector to change its attitude and/or to take a particular action. One example is Greenpeace.

Comment There are many other examples, such as Friends of the Earth, Shelter, the National Society for the Prevention of Cruelty to Children, Amnesty International, etc.

ANSWERS

Exam Practice: Answers and Comments

QUESTIONS TO TRY (page 150)

The answers provided are ones that would score full marks. Check your own answers against them. Where a question is level marked, look carefully at the mark scheme so that you know what you need to do to raise your answer to the top level, if it is not currently a full mark answer.

Q1 a Two advantages of being a sole trader are that there are few legal requirements to set up in business and that limited capital is necessary.

b A main disadvantage would be difficulty in obtaining a bank loan. Banks are less willing to lend to small businesses, as they cannot recoup their losses if the business fails. There is a high risk of failure because small businesses are competing with large organisations and supermarkets. They do not get the large discounts from suppliers enjoyed by large companies. It is difficult to expand because one individual can do only a certain amount of work.

c Unlimited liability means that a sole trader is totally responsible for the debts of the business. Liability is not limited to the business but extends to all his/her possessions. He/She could therefore lose his/her home, possessions and money.

Examiner's comments
- In part a), one point will be awarded for each advantage stated. You could also have mentioned:
  - easy to set up as a sole trader;
  - can make own decisions;
  - small business flexible so owner can change products or activities;
  - sole trader keeps all the profits.
- For part b), you need to provide a fairly complete description of the main disadvantage to obtain full marks. The four marks allocated to the question indicate that detail is required.
- For part c), you need to provide both a definition and an explanation to achieve full marks.

Q2 a Her business objectives at the beginning were to establish her business and then to make a profit. She then expanded as far as she intended by employing more staff, moving to larger premises and acquiring regular customers. Her objectives now must be to retain customers, to acquire more clients, either through advertising or through her reputation, and to maintain her reputation.

The main concerns of mass-market retailers will be with growth and sales maximization. If a particular product fails to sell, the loss is greater because many thousands will have been produced, whereas Jo can afford to operate with smaller profit margins, and one loss will not be dramatic. Large firms are also competing permanently for a larger market share because they know that their competitors are always doing so.

b Jo can measure the success of her business by comparing each year's profit with the preceding year's. She can see if her sales have increased, both in terms of money and number of customers. She can see how often her stock has turned over in the year, which will show how satisfactory her choice of stock has been.

Examiner's comments
- Part a would be level marked:
  - Level 1: Basic understanding. The answer consists of at least two simple examples, related to the case study.   1–2 marks
  - Level 2: Clear understanding. The candidate clearly understands the nature of quality goods and the mass market. The examples given in Level 1 are developed.   3–4 marks
  - Level 3: At least three clear and explained examples, illustrating the candidate's understanding and linked to the businesses mentioned.   5–6 marks

Q3 a Two characteristics of leasing are: You never own the item, and if anything goes wrong, the firm is responsible for repairs.

Two features of hire purchase are: You don't own the item until your last payment, and the total cost is high because of the inclusion of interest rates.

b Hire purchase would result In a greater outlay of capital than leasing. Usually, a deposit would have to be paid, and Jo would be responsible for any repairs after the initial guarantee period had expired. With leasing, there would be no initial deposit or responsibility for repairs.

The choice would therefore depend, to a large extent, on how much cash Jo had available. I would recommend Jo leasing initially, as the business is still in its early days. She has also just spent quite a lot on staff and office equipment. Once she is sure that her cash flow is stable, she can move to hire purchase as long as she has only leased the van for a fairly short time, e.g. a year.

Q4 a A niche market.

b i) Commodity market: tea

ii) Industrial markets: computer parts

iii) Financial markets: banking

iv) Consumer markets: clothes

v) Niche markets: specialised sports equipment

vi) Traditional markets: market stalls

c Product-oriented goods are those which are produced where the main aim is to make high-quality goods without thinking first of the market. After they are made, manufacturers will think about where they are to sell them. Product-oriented goods usually have a high reputation, so manufacturers do not need to consider their market so much. Most product-oriented goods are in the commodity markets, where the quality of the raw material is of prime importance.

Market-oriented goods are produced with the market in mind first. Manufacturers will find out what is required and then design their product to meet that demand.

d Industrial markets have become more market oriented because the manufacturers of these goods, such as machine tools, which had to adhere to a technical specification, now have to consider specific requirements of particular manufacturers. Nowadays, machines and equipment have to be adapted to meet the needs of people who are producing special products, or one-off items. For example, a manufacturer of computer software may be providing software packages for local government. He will need to identify the particular needs of this market, which will be different from the private consumer market. Special packages may be needed for dealing with council tax, social services and housing. An example of an organizational market is an exhibition.

- Other possible examples for part b):
  - Commodity markets: iron, zinc, gold, silver, grain, wheat, sugar, tin.
  - Industrial markets: factory machinery, containers, lorries, car parts or components.
  - Financial markets: insurance, money markets, foreign exchange markets, stock exchange.
  - Consumer markets: food, consumer durables, single-use goods, consumer services from hairdressing to legal advice.
  - Niche markets: any specialised goods or services, for example relating to sportswear, holidays, education, ethnic groups, religious bodies, antiques, ski boots.
  - Traditional markets: market halls, auctions, car-boot sales.
- Part d of this question would be level marked:
  - Level 1: Simple understanding of the meaning of industrial markets and what they are composed of. 　　　　　　　　1–2 marks
  - Level 2: Explanation of the way in which industrial markets have become market oriented. 　　　　　　　　3–4 marks
  - Level 3: Detailed description of the way in which industrial markets have become market oriented and appreciation of the reasons for this development. 　　　　　　　　5 marks
  - One mark for example of an organizational market. 　　　　　　　　6 marks
- Other organizational markets might include publicity and advertising; public relations; arranging conferences; organising events for large firms and companies, such as anniversaries, commemorative events, celebrations; specialized advice such as investment and pension funds.

Q5 The Internet is a good way of advertising the business. She could have an eye-catching home page which would attract browsers. There could be a picture of the interior of the shop and a display of the goods.

It would not cost her a lot. Her Internet Service Provider would give her 25Mb of web space free of charge. Although she is catering mainly for local trade, people from all over the world could visit the website. Her customers could send her an e-mail to ask any questions, and she could e-mail back with the answer.

Not all ISPs provide 25 Mb of free web space, and many people are afraid to carry out financial transactions on the Internet, because they fear their credit-card numbers may be stolen. Mastercard and Visa have introduced a new system – SET (Secure Electronic Transaction) – to make customers feel secure enough to use their credit cards for online purchases.

Examiner's comments

- This question would be level marked:
  - Level 1: Simple description of the uses of the website on the Internet. 　　1–3 marks
  - Level 2: Explanation of the value of a website with understanding of the benefits to be gained. 　　　　　　　　4–6 marks
  - Level 3: Detailed assessment of the benefits of a website and an appreciation, with examples, of its relevance to the case study. 7–8 marks

Published by HarperCollinsPublishers Ltd
77-85 Fulham Palace Road
London W6 8JB

www.**Collins**Education.com
On-line support for schools and colleges

© HarperCollins*Publishers* Ltd 2003

First published 2003
10 9 8 7 6 5 4 3 2
ISBN 0 00 713623 4

British Library Cataloguing in Publication Data
A catalogue record for this book is available from the British Library.

Edited by Catriona Watson-Brown
Production by Jack Murphy
Series design by Sally Boothroyd
Index compiled by Julie Rimington
Book design by Ken Vail Graphic Design, Cambridge
Printed and bound in China

Acknowledgements
The Author and Publishers are grateful to the following for permission to reproduce photographs (T = Top, B = Bottom, C = Centre, L = Left, R = Right):

ADIA Alfred Marks 106; AGCO Ltd 91T; Boosey & Hawkes MI Ltd 91B; Patricia Briggs 21, 67B; British Bakeries Ltd 88T, 88B; CenterCore Systems Ltd 118; Cate Coles Fashion Design 122T; Collins Technology Archive 132B; Consumers' Association 131; Corbis 1BL&R, 6, 59CB, 116; London Docklands Development Corporation 132T; The Dairy Council 67T; Nestlé UK Ltd 79; Sally & Richard Greenhill 135, 136; Safeway 80, 124; SK Drawing Services 122B; Stone/Getty Images 59CT, 59B; Telegraph/Getty Images 1TL&R, 8, 59T; Walkers Snack Foods 69; Wallis Tomlinson Ltd 72.

Illustrations
Gecko Limited 2, 19, 25, 71, 72, 73, 74, 138

Every effort has been made to contact the holders of copyright material, but if any have been inadvertently overlooked, the Publishers will be pleased to make the necessary arrangements at the first opportunity.

You might also like to visit:

www.**fireandwater**.com
The book lover's website

INDEX

quality control managers 21, 22
questionnaires in research 64
quotations, forms for 120

R&D (research and development) 92
Race Relations Act (1976) 104
radar beams 125
radio advertising 73
radio-frequency terminals 124
rail freight 136
ranges, product 69
ratios 48-9, 50-1, 56-8
  acid test 57
  current 56-7
  gross profit margin 48
  net profit to sales 50-1
  return on capital employed 58
  stock turnover 48-9
  working capital 56-7
raw materials 3, 4
  buying 87
  and location 136
RDCs (regional distribution centres)
  80-1, 124
receivers in communication 116
recessions 95
recommendation in recruitment 106
recruitment 105-9
  induction programmes 111, 118
reducing-balance method 36
redundancy 111, 125
  in cost cutting 29, 32
  and IT 126
  in mergers and takeovers 19
redundancy pay 104, 111
references in recruitment 107, 108
regional assistance 133
regional distribution centres (RDCs) 80-
  1, 124
regional selective assistance 133
Registrar of Companies 43
regulators, privatized utility 130
religion in market segmentation 61
repair costs 28
reports 118
  annual reports and accounts 43, 120
research
  customers in 16
  and development (R&D) 92
  market research 63-5
reserves on balance sheets 54
results, payment by 97-8
retail finance 83
retail funds 83
retailing and retailers 80-2
  in distribution 77, 80-1
  IT used by 124
  location 134-5, 136
  out-of-town 80, 81, 135
  see also shops
retained profit 35

return on capital employed (ROCE) 58
revaluation reserve 54
revenue
  in breakeven analysis 33-4
  and cash flow 32
  on trading accounts 46
  see also sales, total; turnover
revenue expenditure 27
rights, employee 95
risk 14, 18
  and franchising 10
  and partnerships 8
  and sole proprietors 6
robots in production 123
  see also automation
ROCE (return on capital employed) 58
royalty payments 10

sacrifice of alternatives 17
safety see health and safety
salaried staff 98, 100
  see also white-collar employees
salaries 98
  see also pay
sale of assets
  for cost cutting 29
  as source of finance 35
sale and leaseback 41
sales, cost of 46, 47
  and stock turnover ratio 48
sales departments, functions of 23
sales (mark-downs) 71
sales promotions 75
sales, total 46
  in breakeven analysis 33-4
  and cash flow 32
  in gross profit margin 48
  in net profit to sales ratio 50-1
Sale and Supply of Goods Act (1994) 130
sampling in research 64
saturation phase 68
scanners 124
secondary production 3, 4
secondary research 63-4
security needs 94
segmentation, market 60-2
selection process (recruitment) 107-8
self-employment 6
  see also sole proprietors
self-esteem 94
self-fulfilment 94
selling price in breakeven analysis 33-4
semi-variable costs 27-8
senders in communication 116
senior managers 22
servers, computer 118
services 1, 3
  financial services 3, 38
  and market segmentation 61
  and Trades Description Act 130
  see also tertiary production

sex see gender issues
Sex Discrimination Act (1975) 103
shareholders 5, 12, 13
  accounts for 43
  annual general meetings for 119
  dividends for 12, 35
shareholders' funds on balance sheets 54
share premium account 54
shares 12, 13
  dividends 12, 14, 35
  electronic dealing 125
  as a fringe benefit 100
  price, and business size 17
  from privatizations 43
  trading 13, 41, 44, 83
  value of, on balance sheets 54
shift premium payments 97
shops
  small shops 81-2
  supermarkets 67, 80-2
  use of IT 124
  see also retailing and retailers
short lists of candidates 108
short-term finance 42
short-term work 95
sick-pay schemes 100
sideways communication 115
single-status employment 103
single union agreements 103
sites and premises 134-5
sites, Web 121
skimming price 71
sleeping partners 8
small businesses 26, 61, 82
  and banks 84
  government loans to 40
  and market research 65
  shops 81-2
  see also sole proprietors
Small Firms Loans Guarantee Scheme 40
social audits 139
social class 60
social costs and benefits 139-41
social needs 94
social responsibilities 134-41
socio-economic groups 60
software 118
  see also IT
sole proprietors 6-7
  accounts 43
  drawings 35, 50
  location 135
  sources of finance 40-1
  see also small businesses
sources of finance 35-42
span of control 22
special offers 75
specialization 4, 23, 24, 88
spoken messages 116, 117, 118-19
spreadsheets, computer 118
staff bulletins or magazines 118